Disguises
of LOVE

A Collection of Meditations and Prayers

Eddie Askew

By the same author:
A Silence and a Shouting
Many Voices, One Voice
No Strange Land
Facing the Storm
Breaking the Rules
Cross Purposes
Slower than Butterflies
Music on the Wind
Edge of Daylight (Memoirs)
Talking with Hedgehogs

Published by
The Leprosy Mission International
80 Windmill Road, Brentford
Middlesex TW8 0QH, United Kingdom
First published 1983, first colour edition 2002

Editorial and Design by Craft Plus Publishing Ltd.
53 Crown Street, Brentwood, Essex CM14 4BD

Printed and bound in Spain by Bookprint, S.L. - Barcelona
A catalogue record for this book is available from the British Library.
ISBN 0 902731 22 X

Cover picture (printed in full on title page): Scottish Farm, Iona, *Watercolour*

The Leprosy Mission (TLM) is an international Christian charity caring for people affected by leprosy. TLM was founded in 1874 by Irishman Wellesley Bailey. It is motivated and inspired by Christ's ministry of compassion to people suffering from leprosy. Today TLM is working in 28 countries, treating more than 200,000 people personally affected by leprosy.

TLM aims to meet the physical, mental, social and spiritual needs of people affected by leprosy, whilst working towards the eventual eradication of the disease. The Mission has 2,300 field staff and works both directly, through its own hospitals and programmes, and in partnership with churches, voluntary agencies, patient organisations, governments and international organisations to meet the broad-ranging needs of people affected by leprosy. It is supported by voluntary contributions of churches, support groups and individuals around the world and has an international budget of £10 million.

Leprosy is a medical condition affecting millions of people, 90% of whom live in the developing world. If left untreated, it causes disability and even blindness. It is not hereditary but is caused by a bacillus which attacks the nerves under the skin causing inflammation and anaesthesia. It is not a punishment for sin! Over 95% of the world's population is naturally immune and, after only a few days of treatment with Multidrug therapy (MDT), patients are no longer infectious. Since the 1980s over 10 million people have been cured with MDT, but the challenge remains as teams are still detecting over 600,000 new cases each year.

TLM Trading is a wholly owned subsidiary of The Leprosy Mission and raises funds for TLM's work through mail-order selling. The long-term aim is to offer more items made by people affected by leprosy in order to help give employment and dignity.

TLM Trading Limited
P.O. Box 212
Peterborough
PE2 5GD
United Kingdom

Please use your local Leprosy Mission address if you prefer, see page 88.

Please
affix
stamp

The Leprosy Mission Response Card

Eddie Askew is a popular Christian author and artist. His books raise funds for The Leprosy Mission to help people affected by leprosy. They are available from The Leprosy Mission in your own country or from TLM Trading Limited in the UK as well as most good Christian book shops.

Titles by Eddie Askew	Order Code
A Silence and a Shouting	03001
Disguises of Love	03002
Many Voices One Voice	03003
No Strange Land	03004
Facing The Storm	03005
Breaking the Rules	03006
Cross Purposes	03000
Slower than Butterflies	03024
Music on the Wind	03025
Edge of Daylight (Hardback)	03026
Edge of Daylight (Paperback)	03027
Talking with Hedgehogs	03028
Talking with Hedgehogs (audio cassette)	20201

Titles by Hilary Faith Jones – with illustrations by Eddie Askew

Hilary Faith Jones is a new author writing poetry that gets to the heart of the Christian faith.

Awakenings	03030
Waiting For Jesus	03031
Awakenings (audio cassette)	20250

Title .... Initials .... Surname ....

Address...

Post Code...................... Country ....

TLM Trading Limited, owned by The Leprosy Mission, seeks to create employment by purchasing goods from rehabilitation centres and craft workshops which employ people affected by leprosy. These goods are sold along with gifts, cards and books to raise funds for The Leprosy Mission.

Please send me information about:- (please tick)

- [ ] The Leprosy Mission's mail-order catalogue
- [ ] The Leprosy Mission's work
- [ ] Prayer support
- [ ] Sending a regular gift by automatic payment, standing order, or direct debit to support The Leprosy Mission
- [ ] Tax efficient ways of supporting The Leprosy Mission
- [ ] Service Overseas with The Leprosy Mission
- [ ] Making and amending a Will and leaving a legacy to The Leprosy Mission

Credit card sales and enquiries:
Tel: 01733 239252   Fax: 01733 239258
E-mail address: enquiries@tlmtrading.com

Sudden Sunshine   *Pastel*

To my daughters, Stephanie and Jennifer, whose
humour and love keep me thinking.
And with gratitude, to all my colleagues in the
International Office of the The Leprosy Mission
for their friendship and encouragement.

Introduction

WHEN THIS BOOK was originally published, people were just coming to know Eddie Askew's work. These meditations and prayers were first produced to feature in The Leprosy Mission's newsletter which is distributed to mission workers in many countries. We are thankful that Eddie's words have now been published in book form (this is the second in the series) so that we can all enjoy, find comfort from and use them as part of our spiritual journey.

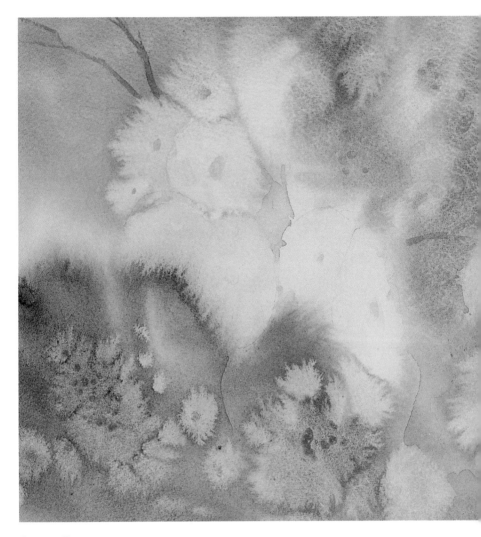

Summer Dreams

These days Eddie's books are well known and well loved. As a result The Leprosy Mission is republishing this volume, along with others in the series, in a new style and with Eddie's own colour illustrations to complement his writing. TLM expects that those who have the original book will find this revisiting of the work like seeing a good friend put on a new outfit; those who do not know the first edition will be able to explore the thought-provoking words while delighting in Eddie's skilful and delicate watercolours and pastels.

Eddie Askew and his wife Barbara served in India at the Purulia Leprosy Hospital for 15 years and both their daughters were born whilst they were there. Consequently, India, and its people, hold a special place in their lives. When the family returned to England, Eddie became International Director of The Leprosy Mission. He travelled the globe meeting the people who dedicate their lives to the Mission's work. He also met with world leaders to bring to their attention ways to eradicate the disease and help those affected by it.

In 2000 Eddie was awarded the OBE for his services to leprosy relief.

Watercolour

Parish Church, Cirencester

5

Disguises of love

1 John 4:9-12

H AN SUYIN, the author says, "Love is a many-splendoured thing." So it is. Shimmering like crystal, its rainbow beams sparkling, picking up the smallest ray of light and turning life into a rich spectrum of colour. That's the easy bit. That's the sort of love I can accept. That's the love I can identify and rejoice in without effort.

But that's only one part of the whole and, although most of us would happily settle for that much, we have to turn the page to continue the story on the other side. The other side is, at first glance, more sombre. In the shadows the lines are softer, less bright; sometimes hard to see. Instead of the glow of colour, the darkness seems only to throw back a reflection of suffering. The arms held open in welcome become pale arms drawn tense on a cross. Rich reds dull into spilt blood. The song of joy becomes a groan of pain.

Yet it's still love. More splendid than the brilliance which dazzles me. It's just harder to recognise because it's not the way I'd paint it. Self-giving love: suffering, dying.

And if I'm going to share the splendour of love then I have to recognise the pain as part of it. Not just as a counterpoint, making the colour more brilliant in contrast with the dark, but as part of its reality.

In the recognition, understanding begins. When pain and disappointment hit me, I may still rebel and protest, but slowly, with infinite patience, God, who is love incarnate, leads me to see that love stands there in the shadows, just as he stands in the light. Not necessarily creating the pain, but working through it with me for good – and slowly I am able to recognise some of the disguises of love. Slowly and hesitantly I begin to understand that his forms are myriad, and that love comes in ways I never thought possible. Love speaks not only in the still small voice, but also in the frightening storm, and in an infinity of guises. The adventure is to recognise him.

Farmer's cottage,
West of Ireland

6

Lord, there are times
when silence seems best.
And yet, when I'm faced with your love,
even with the little I know, I have to speak.
If nothing else, to say thank you.
I don't deserve it.
Now there's an understatement.
Sometimes all I am and do
seems designed to test your love to the limit.
And you go on loving.
Lord, it's breathtaking. Immense.
I hear your voice, carrying crystal clear over the vast plain,
re-affirming life and presence.
A small point of focus in infinity. Infinity of love.
Great enough for all. Small enough for me.

A love that comes to identify, to tell me I belong.
That comes to strengthen, to tell me it's mine.
That comes to comfort with the knowledge that you care.
A love that comes to challenge and discipline at the point of stress.
That stretches me nearly to breaking point and makes me grow.
That faces me, in searching, insistent strength,
with the pain of truth I'd rather not see.
That strips my illusions and leaves me trembling, naked,
in the cold wind of honesty.
The love that fights me as I struggle to preserve the lies I love
from the buffeting storm of your Spirit.

And through it all,
a love that holds me, firm and close.
Making me aware, in the eye of the cyclone, of your peace.
And in the wind-drop of understanding,
my ears still ringing, eyes still smarting, from the gale,
I recognise your love.
In the glacier wind as in the valley breeze.
Seeing, as in the crackling flash of brief lightning,
brilliant and clear,
some of the disguises of your love.
Lord, I know there's more,
but I'm not ready for it yet.

A landmark of love

I Peter 2:4-10

IN HIS NOVEL, *The Spire,* William Golding takes us back into the lives and tensions of people involved in building a medieval cathedral tower. It is to be higher than any built before. The architect and builder have no firm knowledge on which to base design and calculations, no mathematics of structural stresses, no textbooks. It is an exploration, a path ploughed into the unknown.

One day, the Dean, who is the inspiration and force behind the work, climbs up with the workmen and looks out over the countryside from the great height already reached. He sees people far away and far below moving over the crest of a slope and walking straight down the fields towards the city. They ignore the old meandering paths, and move straight towards the new landmark, the spire. In a moment of vision he sees how feet will cut new tracks through the countryside, drawn by the cathedral. 'He understood how the tower was laying a hand on the landscape, altering it, dominating it, enforcing a pattern that reached wherever the tower could be seen, by sheer force of its being there.' He had dreamed and planned the spire, but hadn't understood how the effects would reach out, changing a whole pattern of life. We try to predict the process of cause and effect, but so much works out in ways we can't foresee.

The master builder becomes frightened of the immensity of the work. The Dean pushes him on, saying, "You'll build it to the top. You think those are your own hands, but they aren't. You think it's your own mind that's been working, nagging at the problem ... but it isn't." And the Spirit moves them on, working out his purposes through the effort and sweat, even through the bewilderment of people who see only the next step ahead, and take it in faith.

In Jesus, God planted a landmark which reorientates the whole of life, much more fundamentally than the cathedral spire. From the meandering tracks and the uncertainty of the next corner, a straight path, its end clear, leads not to a stone tower but to a living kingdom of love. And it is replanted in individuals, affecting them in different ways, changing the pattern of life and relationships. It pushes us, like the cathedral builders, into an exploration of the unknown; stretching us to the limits of our comprehension and faith, sometimes frightening us. But it is not just our hands, our minds. In the baby of Bethlehem, God released into the world a power beyond anything before or since – the power of love. The weakest, strongest, quickest killed and longest living power ever known. And that is the power we work with.

Lord, I look to you
for orientation.
Without you the landscape is confusing.
My sense of direction is weak,
and, more often than not,
I move in circles,
ending where I began.
And with less energy.

I admire the spire; its builder.
The urge to glorify you
which placed one stone on another
and raised a landmark.
I praise you
whenever I enter an old church
and remember
long centuries of faithful prayer.

But Lord, your landmark is love.
More vulnerable than any tower.
Weaker yet stronger than any stone.
Enduring, when all else fails.
Invisible,
yet clear to see with eyes of faith.
Shape me, Lord,
as the mason shapes his stone,
with firm blows lovingly aimed,
that I may take my place,
a living stone in your temple.

Lord, I base my life
on the compass point of your love.
Lead me to it
whatever road I take.
And help me point others to it,
by all I do and say.

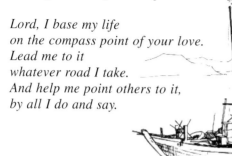

Floating Home, Hong Kong

Giving and receiving

John 13:1-9

"I T IS MORE blessed to give than to receive" and often – alas – easier. In its context it's true enough, but often it's wrenched out of context and used to justify the ungracious way in which some folk refuse offers of help. "Oh! Really you shouldn't have." "No, I can't possibly accept it." Sometimes the words are part of a ritual of politeness, but they often conceal a pride which can't accept the idea of help, and which won't admit the need for it.

I was reading the story of the footwashing incident in the Gospels. During supper, after which Jesus had spelled out his sacrifice in the bread and wine at the table, and the disciples had responded so appallingly in the dispute over who would be greatest in the kingdom, Jesus took the basin and began to wash their feet. It was an action Peter couldn't accept. I can identify with Peter; I often can. I find it as easy as Peter did to profess my loyalty, as hard as Peter did to live it. Perhaps already ashamed of the dispute, realising that Jesus had needed a more sensitive response to the burden he was sharing with them, Peter couldn't take the idea of Jesus doing more for him. "No, Lord, you shall never wash my feet, I can't accept that ..." And Jesus responds, "If I don't wash you, you are not in fellowship with me" (John 13:8 NEB).

Unless we learn to receive we are not really one with him. And this goes right through our relationship with God. It's a strange thing. On one level we take Christ's sacrifice as his supreme gift to us, we acknowledge our weakness and our need for his grace and power, but then on a different level we rush around madly trying to earn it all by frantic service. It's as though, like Peter, we can't bear the thought of not deserving it. We want a good credit rating to justify all that Jesus has invested in us. And in the friction at the interface between these opposing ideas (to use today's jargon), we are ill at ease, and deeply unsure.

Maybe I've got it wrong, but I don't think so. The reality of Christ's living in us will show in what we do as well as in what we are. The two can't be separated, but it isn't his compulsion that drives us ragged into the ground through overwork. We do that ourselves. We need to accept quietly and joyfully all that Christ had done for us, realising that his fellowship doesn't depend on our immediately giving something back. The same goes for our personal relationships. Other people need to feel wanted too. If we are always doing things for them, how can they experience the joy of giving? If it's always one sided how can either of us be whole? It is, in this context, as blessed to receive as to give, and perhaps more so. Independence sounds great, but it's in interdependence that the richness of our humanity lies.

Lord, in the quietness
I feel your love washing over me.
Lifting the dust, cleansing the dirt.
I feel your hands, firm,
gentle, with the towel.
I can take that.
What I find hard, too hard to take,
is seeing you kneeling
at my feet.

I can understand, Peter,
I can feel his shock as he looked down,
looked down on you.
To find you on the floor.
The protests rise in my throat, as they did in his.
I can accept a high and mighty God,
it fits the pattern of the world I live in.
A world of yes sir, no sir, three bags full sir.
But to see you, Lord,
there, at my feet. That's hard.
It makes me uncomfortable.
I feel threatened. It's too great a gift.
I want to lift you up
and put you back on the pedestal.
That's where God belongs.

And yet I think I see what you're saying.
That in a world where everything has to be paid for
your love is free.
That in your kingdom, privilege counts –
for nothing.
And that all the values of the world
turn upside down at your touch.
Lord, it's your gift. It's so great,
so different from anything I've known,
it has no price tag.
I can't save for it, can't earn it,
can't even bargain for it. Just accept it.

Lord, give me the humility
to accept your humility.

A spirit of wisdom

Acts 6:1-7

THE EARLY CHURCH in Jerusalem was a commune, or something rather like one, with everything held in common. (It didn't last long, Christians are not yet perfect.) A quarrel developed over the care of needy people. After discussion, everyone agreed to give responsibility for this work to particular individuals. Those chosen were to be 'full of the Spirit and of wisdom' (Acts 6:3). I suppose I'd always assumed the two went together; that if your life was filled with the Spirit, wisdom came automatically. But if that were so, then why the emphasis? Why say 'and of wisdom' at all? It could have been taken for granted.

Then I began to look around and relate what this bit of the Bible was saying to life as I know it and, as so often happens, the Bible was right. The two things – Spirit and wisdom – don't always go together. A lot of Christians have little wisdom in dealing with their fellow humans, or in resolving problems within their lives. Enthusiasm, but not wisdom.

Now, wisdom comes from the Holy Spirit, for he is the 'Spirit of truth'. The psalmist tells us that the fear of the Lord is the beginning of wisdom and adds 'and they who love by it grow in understanding'. But it takes time, effort and nurture, as does all growth. It demands, too, that we give up our soft cushion of simple assumption that everything will come right if only we love one another. I've met folk who have no patience with organisation or administration, who see it as unnecessary and a waste of time. "If you have the Spirit you can forget about the rest. He'll guide you," they say. Hard experience suggests otherwise. These are often the people who live by crisis, staggering from one problem to the next, many of which could have been resolved, even avoided, by thoughtfulness and concern for others. Wisdom, to me, has a lot to do with concern for others. It's about understanding, gauging human reactions, and planning so that stress is reduced as far as it can be. It can't be eliminated totally. Taking decisions often produces stress, and we have to live with it. Good management isn't the imposition of bureaucracy, but the development of a strong and reasonably secure framework within which we expand and develop our ideas and concerns.

And without it? Chaos. Conflicting demands, half-baked ideas, misunderstanding and extra stress. People often kick against organisational constraints, shouting for freedom. Sometimes they are right, but more often it is the very organisation they protest against that props them up and gives them both the freedom and the support on which to build. It isn't a denial of the Spirit's guidance to think ahead and plan; it's a use of our God-given gifts of mind and thought.

Lord, they were close to you
those people in Jerusalem.
Close in time,
although I don't think that matters
because in your eternity, outside time,
you're just as close to me.
Sold their homes and land,
burnt their boats –
I know you're smiling
at the mixed metaphor –
committed themselves to you.
And yet, they didn't agree.

I've heard it before, Lord,
experienced it.
I've known the enthusiasm, the joy,
slowly drifting into dissension.

Lord, in my eagerness to share,
in my desire to get things right,
help me to recognise
the sensitive toes around me.
Sensitive from past treading on,
apprehensive with future fear.
And, while those raw nerves
mustn't stop me from doing what's right,
help me to see clearly what is right.
And the most loving way of doing it.
Walking with you,
as I listen and learn,
hopefully, Lord, hopefully,
let your wisdom rub off onto me.
Your sensitivity to others' needs.
Help me to learn
that spirit and wisdom and love
must go together,
and that to combine them all
takes effort and perception.
Understanding.
Help me only to tread on their toes,
as I would like them to tread on mine!

...make me sparkle again
with a newness of purpose.

Norfolk Cottage

Watercolour

Taking care

Mark 12:28-34

I'VE A FRIEND who is a skilled musician. He plays the flute. I met him recently and, after the usual questions about health and work, he told me of a shock he'd just had. He was soon to play in a local concert and was getting down to serious practice. The other day he sat down to play but nothing happened. No sound. He tried again. He checked the flute. No music. I can imagine the shock! Then quietly, he began to analyse what he was doing and realised what had gone wrong. The flute was all right, but he'd been getting careless. Instead of sitting or standing straight, his arms just so, he'd begun to slump. His hands weren't right, and had gradually twisted the angle at which he held the flute. And when he blew over the hole in the mouthpiece, the angle was wrong. The music had gone. I met him again last Sunday. "How's the flute?" I asked. "Just great, I've corrected the stance, I'm back in business!"

It's an interesting metaphor on Christian living. It's not that we give up, or reject it. We just get careless. We still go to church, pray, read the Bible, but without the attention we used to have. We live without really thinking, and suddenly we are shocked into the realisation that nothing is happening. We blame the flute, the prayer, the faith, but so often the answer's in our own hands. We need to get back to the discipline of thoughtful, not thoughtless, discipleship. It takes effort, as well as time. It needs singleness of purpose, kept clean and polished against the patina of use.

Jesus answered, "The Lord our God, the Lord is one. Love the Lord your God with all your heart and with all your soul and with all your mind and with all your strength" (Mark 12:29-30).

And remember he goes on to tell us to love our neighbours as ourselves.

Pavement Dwellers, Calcutta

"Don't shoot the pianist, he's doing his best."
Not always true, Lord.
It's not always the piano that's wrong.
Nor the flute.
Sometimes it's the player.
Me.
When there's no music between you and me,
when the melody's gone,
the harmony shattered,
it's not the instrument,
it's me.

Not that I've given up totally, Lord.
Not that I've rejected you and your love.
It's just that I'm half asleep, careless,
not standing upright in your presence,
my dedication dusty and dormant in a dark corner.
Wake me up, Lord, from self-satisfaction.
Rescue me from the trap of complacency.

Don't weaken your demands on me,
just help me strengthen my response.
Wash off the grime of long usage
and make me sparkle again in newness of purpose.
Open my eyes, Lord.
It's happened before – thank you for your patience –
open my eyes
to the wonder of life with you,
to the joy of life in the community of your church.
Make me a blessing to them,
to those I love.
Make me into someone
it's good to be around.
Like you.

Start the music again, Lord.
And put in a few grace notes.

Energy renewed

Revelation 21:5-7

W E HAD a holiday in Switzerland. We headed for the mountains, up to Grimentz. We drove, with care, up to and past the Moiry Dam, right to the foot of the glacier. It was bleak but beautiful, the cold air diesel-free, the sun flashing on the ice, the white peaks against the deep blue sky hard-edged as a modern painting. Rock, ice, sunshine – a different world.

Glaciers are awesome. Great sheets of ice, hundreds of feet thick, stretching down the mountain from the heights of perpetual snow, solid as the rock underneath. Yet that's deceptive because glaciers are on the move. Those millions of tons of ice are sliding down all the time, often hundreds of feet a year, under the weight of continuing new deposits of snow. In places the ice moves smoothly, in others it's a wild jumble of broken crevasses. It moves down until the warmth of lower altitude melts the ice, and small streams coalesce into the urgency of waterfall and mountain river.

First the water runs free, and then it is channelled through the pipes of hydroelectric projects, where its energy spreads out through electric cables to heat homes, run trains and turn factory machinery. The energy is God-given and continually renewed. Properly harnessed, it transforms life, powering communities.

High on the mountain, the glacier is constantly topped up. So God's power is never-ending, always available. It's dynamic. The glacier is in continual movement and change; change unstoppable and necessary. Otherwise, the water supply would dry up, the electric cables become useless monuments to early promise and dead hope. So, change has to be seen as growth and life. "Behold," promises the Lord, "I am making everything new" (Rev 21:5). "I am making" used in a continuous tense.

Things are not always easy. I imagine the stress at the interface of rock and ice, the stone gradually smoothed and moulded by pressure and friction, corners and hard edges eroded. And when things go wrong, when you press the switch and the light doesn't work, it's no use blaming the glacier. The fault lies somewhere within the man-made section; in a pipe or fuse or cable. Or it may be a problem of unequal distribution, or overload created by selfish, unthinking overuse. I've made the point but there is maybe just one more thing worth remembering. The power of God isn't ice-cold and glacial, but glowing and warm and loving, like the sun which melts the ice and starts the whole cycle yet again.

I look at the mountains, Lord.
Cloud veil, shawl of summit snow.
Ice-train down tumbled rocks.
Reflecting the blue infinity of space, far above me.
The psalmist pictured them reaching up to you,
dancing in your presence. Singing for joy.
Full of life. Dynamic.
Filled with your energy.
Energy that powers the earthquake, grows the flower.
Caged in the atom, latent in the gene,
moving, working, according to your law.

Lord, I feel small.
It's not an original thought,
but at the foot of the mountain of your power
I acknowledge my weakness, my dependence.
But then, before you become too remote in my thoughts,
I see the evidence of your love.
As the ice moves down the mountain,
melts, and from the great glacier
channels in rushing stream,
releasing, transforming the energy for my use,
so your love is at work.
Out of your great store
the streams pour out in plenty.
Sustaining, refreshing,
cleansing the dirt, soothing the hurts,
taking my breath away in the freshness of your Spirit.
Making all things new.
Making me new, now.
And, Lord, as I live today and tomorrow,
channel your power
through me to others.
Use me, to show them,
family, and friends, and workmates,
something of the wonder and majesty
I see in you.
Something of the love and energy
which transforms life
and helps us start to live eternity today.

Where was God?

Luke 24:1-9

FEW OF US had heard of Popayan in Columbia, until an earthquake killed 250 people. Many died in the cathedral, when it collapsed on worshippers just before Easter. A question on a radio programme pointed to the irony of people dying because they'd gone to church, and said they'd probably have survived if they'd stayed at home. The unasked question was "And where was God? Why did it happen?"

It's a question many want to ask on Good Friday. "Where was God, to allow Jesus to die?" The answer is that God was on the cross, dying. It wasn't the sacrifice of someone else - something most of us find quite easy to do when faced with decisions – but of himself. The idea of sacrifice, of dying for others in love, of standing firm on principles, is the very structure of Christian belief. It's powerful, and it's tough. And its vindication, the source of strength for us, lies in the reality of the resurrection.

"Remember how he told you ... and on the third day be raised again" (Luke 24:6-7).

The problem is coming to terms with it in the nuts and bolts of daily living. What happens when we suffer for faith, but the 'third day' is delayed for us? Suffering for Christ we accept, in theory, but it gets hard when there is no immediate relief, or justification. Three days, that's OK. But if the sorrow or frustration go on for weeks, for years? It isn't always short term.

Risen Indeed is a book everyone should read. It's by Michael Bordeaux, published by Darton, Longman and Todd and it's a glowing study of Christian life in the USSR, and is easy and inspiring reading. He describes an Easter in Moscow, and the strength of personal faith among worshippers in a crowded Orthodox church (but ... Orthodox? I thought they were just ... Careful, watch those glib labels!).

"How could they be so sure?" I asked myself. The answer always came back: they have trodden the way of the cross to the hill of Calvary. Their suffering ... stripped them of everything ... imprisoned ... dear ones died ... Today's policies consistently make the ordinary Christian a second-class citizen ... They do not debate the resurrection; they have experienced its reality in their own lives. They have not preserved the faith in hostile surroundings; it has preserved them.

It's this experience which makes faith strong in adversity, able to live in the post-Good Friday loneliness with hopes delayed, because they are not delayed, not really. The hope and justification is not that suffering will end, true though that is, but in the living reality of Emmanuel: 'God with us', now. It's a strength which holds us up in times of loneliness and frustration. Ulrich Schaffer, the poet, writes*:

Sometimes ... my cry ... is
whipped up into an unfeeling universe ...
and then I am afraid ...
that my cry will echo back
and come crashing over me
magnified a thousand times
devastating my life in a cyclone of frenzy
because you have not heard.
But then the silence in the dead of night
is filled
and the void at the centre of the heart
turns into a celebration
at your nearness
And I know that you have heard my cry

Yes, he is there, in the frenzied cyclone, the earthquake, the loneliness, the frustration, affirming that the 'third day' has already come, and can be lived today, even in the unresolved questions that fill our minds.

*From his book entitled *Into Your Light,* published by Inter-Varsity Press 1979

Marsh Cottages, Norfolk

21

Lord, I can't get to grips with things.
The world gets out of hand.
At least, it seems that way to me.
All this talk of your perfect timing leaves me a bit uneasy.
I see strange things happening.
Tragic things. Sick things.
People suffering and dying.
People crying and questioning.
And when the church roof falls in on worshippers
it sometimes seems as though
the roof is falling in on my faith.

Suffering is OK in theory.
It sounds fine,
when I can look at it from a distance
and admire the courage and patience of
others.
Yes, with others, it's acceptable,
especially when it's sandwiched
between two thick slices of piety.
It goes down a treat!

But when it comes down to flesh and blood,
to my body and mind,
it's different.
When my hopes are shattered,
when things don't go according to my plan,
when I have to wait
– I don't like waiting, Lord,
and endure – that's even worse,
then I ask you
can you look at your watch again, Lord?
Please?
Can't you speed up the resurrection?

And then I realise that hope
was never buried in the tomb.
It doesn't wait for tomorrow, or the day after.
It's not the time crystal
vibrating so predictably in my quartz watch
that promises hope ahead.
Not the wishing away of hours or days.
Hope is real, hope is now.

Spring Colours

22

Not future God, but present God.
Here. Now.
Sharing. Taking the weight, the stress.
Not watching from the sidelines, but suffering with me.
And while I wish you'd answer more of my questions,
Your presence takes care of them.
Not in logic
but in love.

Watercolour

23

God's purposes

Psalm 40:1-5

I'M SURE GOD can well care for himself, but there are times when I get a bit anxious on his behalf. I worry at the way folk lay the responsibility on him for the evil of the world. The other day, a friend spoke of someone suffering a tragic, serious illness, and then quoted from a psalm: 'Many, O Lord my God, are the wonders you have done. The things you planned for us no-one can recount to you' (Psalm 40:5). The implication was that somehow everything that happens is from God, and that everything that happens, therefore, is for our good. That worries me because, although a common attitude among Christians, it is fatalistic, and it doesn't fit in with my understanding or experience.

Now, let's be careful. First, an affirmation: God's purposes are wonderful, and they are all for our good. But is everything that happens in the world part of God's purposes? The psalmist doesn't say that. In fact, in verse 14 he recognises the presence in the world of people who hurt and destroy, and warns us against them. Second, humbly, I realise that I'm in no position of wisdom to say dogmatically what is, or isn't, God's will. But I believe that we should be similarly careful about attributing particular tragedies to his will. Can anyone, agonising with someone seriously ill – maybe a leprosy patient who has lost health, home and family – tell him "It's God's will"? I'm sure that it's his will that we do everything we can to help put things right, but that's not the same.

Someone is going to remember Romans 8:28 in a moment and remind me that '...in all things God works for the good of those who love him.' That's different, though, and strengthens the point I'm trying to make. It doesn't say that everything that happens in life is good, or is from God. What it implies is that whatever happens, God can work with us towards good, reaching out to create something positive.

As Christians, we must face the reality of the world. We can't delude ourselves over the activity of evil, or pretend that it's all God's will. We don't know why some people suffer much more that others and why some break under it. But we do know that God is with us, even though sometimes we know it only in retrospect. Looking back, we see that, through the suffering, love was at work in one of his many disguises. Love is often hard to recognise, so close to the suffering that he's hard to identify. So hard that we attribute to him the suffering itself, instead of thanking him for his presence and strength. We can find him in and through the suffering, love's disguises slowly dissolving as we recognise his presence. Not necessarily justifying the suffering, but turning it towards good.

Lord, I spend a lot of time
talking to you about myself.
I have so many needs.
Help me today to think of others.

I pray for people weighed down by worry.
Anxious people, who don't know where to turn.
Who don't know whose door to knock on,
bewildered by what life has brought.
Knocked off balance by the suffering and inequality
they meet at every step.
People without choices,
whose only way is down.

Somehow, Lord, in the turmoil of survival,
in the questioning and the doubt,
show yourself to them.
Let them find you, not in the abstract,
not in the smooth words of the practised preacher,
but in a hand held out to help.
In shared tears, and in the silence
that says everything without words.
May they recognise your purposes for them,
and learn that your will for them is good.

Help us, each one of us,
to face things as they are.
And though the world has forgotten the architect's plans,
though the builders ignore the blueprint,
and the foundations shake with every pressure,
shelter us with your presence.
Help us to see you at work
not only in the good days
but in the bad,
and to know, beyond doubt,
not through others' words but our own experience,
that you work together with us.
For good.

Then, Lord, our praise will be real,
our joy deep.

Frustration

Romans 8:26-29

A PROBLEM landed on my desk a few days ago (so what's new?). I tried hard to deal with it. I did a lot of thinking, logical and lateral, if you know what I mean, and praying too. I found a solution, or so I thought. Then, once again, the same problem came back. Very frustrating. I felt fed up and rebellious. Yes, rebellious. Resentful of the demands made on me, frustrated that my efforts weren't working, that things weren't turning out as I'd expected.

It's something we all have to cope with, and while we accept the theory that responsibility brings problems from time to time, we don't find the problems any easier to deal with when we actually face them. The calm, measured judgement sprouts wings and flies away in a flutter of ruffled feathers, leaving a mess of irritation behind. I opened my Bible – not a bad idea, that, we ought to do it more often – and turned to a favourite passage, Romans 8, with its clear, confident assurance that nothing can cut us off from God's love. Another phrase captured my mind, though: 'the Spirit comes to the aid of our weakness. We do not even know how we ought to pray, but through our inarticulate groans the Spirit himself is pleading for us' (Romans 8:26 NEB).

That's just it. I didn't know what to pray for. Angry, frustrated, I had no idea, no glimpse of a road opening out ahead. 'We don't even know how we ought to pray ...' but the Spirit is at work even then. He takes the frustration, the groans, the pain, all those voiceless tensions, wraps his own concern around them like a comforting blanket, and in everything 'cooperates for good with those who love God'. Even while I'm banging my head against the wall, he's at work with me, not waving a magic wand, but strengthening, clarifying and helping me to cope. He 'cooperates for good' in an active, loving, working relationship, taking problems and disappointments and helping me to use them creatively. It rings more true to me than the simple and sometimes misinterpreted assertion of the Authorised Version that 'all things work together for good' with the suggestion that it is automatic and comes almost without trying. Far from it, but it's a great joy and comfort to realise that even when I don't know what to do, when I can't even define the problem clearly, he's at work on it anyway. It still needs both of us – that's what cooperation means – but it also means I'm not on my own. Take that into the day with you. It's far more use than pious resolutions to do better or try harder – the assurance that God is with you, and ahead of you, and within you.

And the problem? You know, I can't actually remember what it was now!

Lord, I've had enough. I've had it up to here.
There are times when I just don't want any more.
When today's problem is just one too many.
I've tried.
I could knock my head against the nearest wall –
or anyone else's head for that matter! It's not fair ...

But who said anything about 'fair'?
It's only children who think the world's fair!
Was the cross 'fair'? Was the agony, the pain, just?
And, anyway, before I ask for a fair world,
maybe I should think again.
If I got what I truly deserved, my just reward,
Maybe I'd have more problems, not less.
It's only the unfairness of the cross
which gives me any hope at all.
It's only the impossible, breathtaking truth
of love on a cross
that gives me any chance of real life.

And, Lord, the great thing is
I don't have to wade through the quicksand of my problems
to reach the safe ground of your love.
You are in it with me.
While I'm screaming and fighting,
while I'm rebellious and just plain scared –
because my anger is really fear –
you're there with me.

Even when I don't know what to do,
when my thrashing about sinks me deeper in the mire,
when I don't even know what to ask for, your Spirit is at work.
On the problem. On me.
Patiently accepting my anger and fear.
Absorbing my puny protests.
Taking the unformed clay of my anguish,
and moulding, sculpting it
into another little piece of your kingdom.

Lord, I can't cope.
But you can.

Living life's problems

John 14:1-9

THE RUBICK CUBE is a plastic puzzle made up of little squares of different colours which can be moved in several directions. The object is to finish with all the reds on one side of the cube, the blues on another, and so on. It can be done, I've seen it done, but I can't do it. I had a wicked thought though, about sabotaging it. What if I peeled off just one little red square and put a blue one in its place? People could click the cube around for ever and never complete it. In an earlier letter, I wrote about oversimplifying problems. Now I write about the danger of oversimplifying solutions. When we're looking at alternative answers to a problem, we assume that one answer is 'right', and the other 'wrong'. That does happen, and successful people are those who make more right decisions of this sort than wrong ones. When you do that, the Rubick cube has all its sides complete, with the right colours in place.

Unfortunately, many problems don't have nice solutions like that. Most difficulties involve people and, when people are involved, often there is no solution which is 'right' for everyone. Whatever the choice made, someone won't like it, and someone may be hurt. We must be sensitive to people's needs but if we spend our lives trying to please everyone we may as well jump off a cliff – it gets rid of the stress more quickly! Often we have to choose between two incomplete solutions. And these choices are difficult to make. That's one reason why organisations have leaders. If answers were easy we wouldn't need leaders to take responsibility and make decisions. It's not that leaders are morally or intellectually superior to the rest, they usually aren't, it's just that someone has to make decisions and they are there to do it.

We must go further, and accept that many problems can't be solved, even partially. They just have to be lived. There's either no solution, or the situation is one we are powerless to change. A hard lesson to learn. The colours on the cube may never match. What about faith and prayer? Yes, they do move mountains (forgive the change of metaphor), but not always. Sometimes faith and prayer are needed to give strength to endure a problem and fit it into the total pattern of our living. Thinking of problems, Carlo Carretto, a monk I've quoted elsewhere, says, 'If God is my Father I shall not go on saying "Why? Why?" Instead ... "You know. You know".'

And that's the clue, I believe. As John Taylor said, "Calvary gives no answers, but it stills our questions, and inspires us to trust his love for God." And that is the way to face the insoluble problems in life; to recognise them, face them honestly, and leave them with him.

Lord, what I really want is a world without problems.
Where everything's easy, and warm, and cosy.
A world I can predict, where riches don't turn to rags at midnight.
A world of harmony and good feelings.
But it's not like that, Lord.
There are wars and rumours of wars.
Pain and exploitation.
Broken lives on rubbish dumps where hope lies bleeding.
Lord, I don't understand the way you do things.
With your power, your wisdom, your love,
couldn't you have done it differently? Made it easier?

No, I don't understand.
All the theology in the world doesn't really answer the question
which bobs up to the surface of my mind again and again.
And yet – if that's the way it is,
with your power, and wisdom, and love –
maybe that's the way it has to be. For now.

It was no easier for Jesus, was it Lord?
And the problems he faced were not of his making.
Not like my little problems.
The molehills that seem like mountains.
His problems took him to the cross.
To pain, to death.
*No, not **to** pain, **to** death,*
Not to, but through.
Because the one thing I know is that he came out on the other side.

Lord, I pray for all who find life hard today.
Help them to hang on to that.
Help them cling to it when faith is low. When they're down.
When life is hard to understand,
and even harder to live.
And help me realise that I don't need to understand –
I probably couldn't anyway.
Help me simply to trust you.
*You **are** my father.*
And when I've said that
I've said it all.
Except thank you.

Golden Summer

Give me the courage
to face the truth, and the
strength to overcome.

A. D. ASKEW

Watercolour

Accepting responsibility

Romans 12:1-2

THERE ARE TIMES when I have a sneaking sympathy for the devil! You may think it misplaced, but he gets blamed for so many things. If anything goes wrong in our work or personal life he gets clobbered with the responsibility. After all we quote 'Your enemy the devil prowls around like a roaring lion looking for someone to devour' (1 Peter 5:8). Very true, but it's all too easy to put the blame for anything and everything on to him. Some time ago, I was visiting a country (which shall be nameless) sharing in business meetings with a group of Christians, many of whom were convinced that the troubles they were facing all stemmed from the Lord's adversary. They were convinced that what they were doing was right and that the devil was stirring things up.

But is it really as simple as that? He may be the devil, but we ought to be honest and fair in our attitude to him! As I reflected on what was happening in those particular meetings, it became clearer that the people should have been blaming themselves. It was poor planning and slack management causing a lot of the trouble. If people had taken more care in gathering information, in thinking through their ideas, and getting together in real discussion a lot of the trouble could have been avoided. It wasn't a case of the right things being done and the devil pushing his way in. It was a case of carelessness and poor preparation which opened the door and invited the devil in. You can still blame the devil for accepting the invitation, but who issued it? Who opened the door?

In a way, of course, he is to blame. We can make him responsible for tempting us into carelessness and bad planning and for taking advantage of the situation, but really we do have to take some responsibility for what we do ourselves. The way we blame the devil sometimes suggests that we have no free will, no resistance, no point of reference for help and strength and that we can't be blamed when things go wrong. That isn't a Christian doctrine. Certainly, things can go wrong through no fault of our own, but not as often as we like to think.

I'm sure the devil doesn't mind being blamed, just as long as things do go wrong. What he doesn't like is our looking at our own mistakes, admitting them, and asking the Lord to help us learn from them and put them right. That's what makes his toes curl up. And it's the way to more effective living, because it's only when we admit to a share in the responsibility that the Lord can step in and strengthen us. So be fair, even to the devil, it may help you in a very real way.

It's hard to be honest, Lord,
especially with myself.
And when people say they never lie
I suspect they're not telling the truth!
It's hard to face up to my own faults.
I'm always looking for a scapegoat.
Someone, something, some happening
on which to lay the blame
for my own mistakes.

Like a child,
fearful of consequences,
"It wasn't me ..."
I'm still doing it.
I blame environment, heredity,
wrong friends, or circumstance.
The devil.

Lord, face me with my own responsibility.
The choice is mine.
It's not just that I make wrong choices.
I do that, I know,
but often I just drift,
sails flapping, rudderless,
in the random winds of carelessness.
Hiding in prayer
from my own laziness.
Side-stepping the demands of thought in a flippant piety
that pretends I'm waiting for your guidance,
when all I'm doing
is avoiding the discipline of hard work.
Lord, I hope I'm not white-washing the enemy.
I just want to make sure
in this rare moment of attempted honesty
that I don't fall again into the mistake
of saying "It wasn't me ..."
It was, Lord, it is.

Give me the courage to face the truth,
and the strength to overcome.

If only things were different

Romans 8:18-25

THERE'S THE STORY of the old farm worker, asked by a tourist for directions to get to the distant town. "Oh! It's a difficult road," he said. "If I were going there I wouldn't start from here." If only things were different. If things weren't so busy, if life wasn't so rough, if only we could see things more clearly, we'd be happier, and able to give more. Most of us waste time and nervous energy wishing things were better, creating fantasies about what we'd do if we could start with a different set of circumstances. But we can't change the rules, we have to accept things as they are, not with the inertia of fatalism but as a creative point of departure. The fatalist accepts things with a shrug of the shoulders and says, "That's how things always are." The Christian starts by accepting, not kicking rebelliously, but saying "OK, that's the way things are, the way people are – now let's see what we can do."

After all, that was the way Jesus did it. Carlo Carretto, one of the Little Brothers of Jesus, writes in his book, *Summoned by Love:*

> Faced with man's poverty, faced with the flood of pain, He did not ask the Father to alter things ... He could have asked for death to be abolished ... He could have asked for Earth to be transformed into an Eden, where no one could ever be hungry again: He did not do so. He could, He the Omnipotent, the Well-Beloved, have Himself abolished pain and not endured it Himself: He did not ask for this. The real, the whole reality of the creation, made by God and corrupted by human disobedience and sin, had to be accepted as it was. He had to start from this. To accept it as a mystery. To accept it as supreme self-giving. Jesus bowed His head and accepted reality.

He accepted reality as the starting point for his life and work. Your part of the world, or mine, may at this moment look beautiful or ugly, may be depressing or joyful. Probably it's a puzzling mixture. Whatever it is, that's where you are, and you can only accept it – with thanks if you can, although personally I find St Paul's admonition 'in all things to give thanks' very difficult. It is something I aim for, rather than achieve. We may not like it but that's reality and, having accepted it, we can begin, with love and patience, to transform it. The transformation may not be dramatic. Reality can resist change strongly, but love and patience can inject a note of redemption into many situations. Outwardly, the world carried on much as before after Christ's sacrifice, but the new note was ringing out – transforming lives. And when a life is transformed the view of reality is suffused with an indestructible hope, tested from time to time by doubt and loss of courage – but the answer to the farm worker is "You can get there, from here – you have to!"

It's no dream, no fantasy.
You are here in the world you made.
The living Lord.
Not sitting in the sky,
remote, untouched.
But here, sharing it with me.
Sharing the pain and disappointment.
Sharing the joy and the love.

Lord, help me to see you
standing there.
Help me to understand
that pain is only one face of reality.
Help me to realise
that laughter and friendship and love
are part of your cleansing,
and just as real
as the rest.
Help me to feel the reality
of your love.
Its power, its strength.
Joy bubbling in me
from your eternal springs of life.
I hear cries of pain.
But I also hear birdsong,
the whispers of lovers.
The laughter of children.
The voices of friends.
And in the voices
your voice.

Thank you, Lord.
I can face reality
with you.

Paro Valley, Bhutan

Good news in the present tense

Hebrews 13:1-9

I FEEL A BIT uncomfortable when people who have been Christians for years insist on telling their conversion experiences. It's not the stories that make me uncomfortable, but the thought that they ought to have something much more recent to communicate about their Christian life. A poet commented:

Your holy hearsay is not evidence:
Give me the good news in the present tense.
The living truth is what I long to see.
I cannot lean upon what used to be.
Show me how
the Christ you talk about
is living now.

The good news in the present tense. Something seen, not in the stories of half a generation ago, but in those of today. Tell people what happened this morning, or the day before, because that's the living faith of our relationship with Christ now. The Christian life is for living, not just remembering. It's an experience of immediacy – not in the sense of undisciplined and thoughtless action, but in living with Christ today, rather than with the memory of what used to be. I'm not decrying history – it can often help to make sense of what's happening today – but we can't live our lives on it. The Christian faith is based on an historic event, the life and death of Jesus. The history of God's dealing with men and women recorded in the Old Testament helps us understand it; but life is NOW. The remembrance of past blessings can strengthen us as individuals, but for others Christ is relevant if he is shown as the one who can change life today. That's what the poet pleads for. A picture of Jesus changing the lives of those who preach him. I remember a preacher saying, "I wish I lived up to my sermons". We all fall short, of course, but the only relevance in our lives is the love we show, reflecting the love of God in Jesus Christ.

It's that which people recognise, however dimly, and it's that alone which authenticates both our claims and our living. More, it is that love which Christ will recognise in us. '... and love himself shall come and bend over, and catch his likeness in you'. Not a fading old photograph's reminder of a reality long gone, but the immediacy of a reflection in deep water, a likeness which lasts as long as he is with us. It's the way we live today that counts – and that's what scares me! I can remember yesterdays I lived usefully and well; I can make promises for tomorrow; but what about 'the good news in the present tense'?

Lord of today, I'm here, waiting.
Today, like any other day,
yet like no other day that ever was.
Unique, as I am unique.
Different.
The routine, the well-trodden path, is there.
Yet each day is punctuated by small surprises.
And today brings its share
of smiles and sudden laughter,
of irritation and sharp surges of anger.
Fast-moving clouds and sunshine-bursts,
scudding across the landscape. Light and shadow.

Lord, today is your gift to me.
Help me turn it into my gift to you.
Each today pushes back the past into history,
and in the long perspective
I can see your hand at work.
For good. For my good.
And from that view
I can turn to face the prospect of today.

Tomorrow is obscure.
But from that lookout point of past mercies,
I can leave it, again, in your hands.
Knowing that you are the same,
yesterday, today, and forever.

But today is my concern.
Good news in the present tense.
Not just for me, Lord –
although in honesty that's where my interest begins –
but for those with whom I live and work and talk.
Make me an instrument for good.
A small focus of your healing
in a worried world.
I thank you for yesterday.
I leave tomorrow in your hands.

Today is yours and mine.

Golden Morning

Lord, the light still shows me
you are here.

Watercolour

Looking for good

John 1:1-14

H IGH ON MY TV viewing list was M*A*S*H*. I can never remember the full title, but it was a long running series based on the work of a US Army field hospital, just behind the front line of war. Somehow, and in a quite brilliant way, it combined the violence of war with real comedy. It took you from side-splitting laughter to tragedy and back in seconds without ever being 'sick' in idea. There was a very poignant moment in one episode.

Through an innocent remark in a child's letter, one of the leading surgeons is brought face to face with the fact that his life-saving work can be interpreted as repairing wounded fighting men to send them back to war to fight and kill again – or be killed. He had seen his work as life-giving; remedying, rather than adding to, destruction. He is close to despair until his friend breaks through the bleakness saying, "... the answer is to look for good wherever you can find it."

My mind links this with our latest family visit to a local 'Indian' restaurant. Actually it's run by Bangladeshi Muslims, with whom my wife and I converse in rusty Bengali. We were talking about a political crisis which had led to another Middle East war. The proprietor said, with real feeling, that he found it hard to believe in God in the face of all the evil he sees in the world today. Our answer was to point to the miracle of so much goodness in the world, the goodness we all experience in so many ways, and which would be impossible without God. It's the survival of love in a suffering world which points positively to God, not the presence of evil which denies him.

Wherever we are there is good to be found. (Oh come on now, of course there is, if you look for it.) So often, though, we seem conditioned to look for the bad, to register its image on the photographic plate of experience and enlarge it out of all proportion to the reality. Evil is real, but so is goodness, and we are promised a time when goodness will prevail. Until then we have outbursts of love all around us, including the sunglow of light from the Bethlehem birth, burning warmly through the cold mists of pain and unbelief. It answers the doubts – let's be honest and admit to them – not by closely defined statements of faith but by the almost random flowerings of love in the most unexpected places.
Unexpected? Why should they be unexpected? Maybe if we expected them more we'd find them more often in our companions and co-workers for example. The psalmist knew about the shadow of death, and about enemies, but he looked for goodness and mercy, and expected these things to follow him around for all the days of his life. Read Psalm 23 again, and rejoice.

Lord, it's easy to be discouraged
by all the pain and evil I see in the world.
Easy to grow hard and cynical. Paranoid.
Scanning each friendly word for hidden criticism.
Taking the outstretched hand and wondering
what the other hand holds.
Throwing away the message of love
while I look in the envelope for its letter bomb.

So easy, Lord.
But in the quiet with you
the thought comes.
If evil is so strong
and wrong so powerful,
why is there yet such goodness in the world?

There is one world, not two.
And the world that spins into darkness
is only half a turn from light.
And in the dark itself there are lights.
Flickering candles of hesitant flame,
persistent rhythmic neons of colour,
bright floodlights of electric intensity.
A white shining of hope.
And somehow the darkness has no power to put it out.
'The light shines on in the dark,
and the darkness has never quenched it.'
Lord, thank you for that.
For every glimmer of light and goodness
that falls across my path.
For every rumour of righteousness,
each breath of kindness,
each incandescent glow of particular love in my world.
Thank you.
And as they coalesce,
spilling over into the dark chasms of life,
pools and lakes of shimmering light,
I can see the outline of your love.
Quiet. Persistent. Patient. Indomitable.
Evil may deny your presence, Lord,
but the light still shows me you are here.

Seeds of peace

John 14:27-29

WHEN THE ANGEL told Mary she was to be the mother of Jesus, he said she was highly favoured and that she shouldn't be afraid. 'But Mary was greatly troubled ...' (Luke 1:26-30). As well she might be. The 'favour' to Mary included an unorthodox birth with a question-mark over the father, refugee status in Egypt soon after and, later, the anxiety of seeing her son a penniless, wandering teacher who died an untimely, painful death. We see it differently with hindsight, but I'm trying to look at it through Mary's eyes, at the time. Then the angels spoke of 'peace to men on whom God's favour rests', but did they get it? A few years later, those who believed faced political terror, first from the local authorities and then from the Romans. Jesus is called the 'Prince of Peace'. But do his followers find peace? Is it not rather that they are called to struggle and turmoil?

I'm not suggesting the promise of peace is untrue, but maybe we need to look again at what we understand by 'peace'. In Mary's case, the suggestion is that her peace came through a straightforward, humble acceptance of God's will. "I am the Lord's servant" and that's a lovely simple answer. Unfortunately, many of us make life so complex that we can't make the simple answer (the simple thing may be the most difficult actually to do).

I went to see the Attenborough film *Gandhi* – a magnificent production, written perceptively, acted convincingly. A fine picture of a great man dedicated to his pursuit of truth, and with the courage to follow it wherever it led. From his early experiences of racial tension in South Africa, to the struggle for Independence in India, Gandhi needed all his courage and conviction. His gift to the world was non-violence. He wasn't the first to use it (what about Jesus?), but he was the first modern leader to bring it widely into politics. It isn't meek and mild peaceful protest. It tries to avoid physical violence and killing, but it can be a powerful and compelling force. And it can bring conflict. Gandhi suffered greatly for it, but the film suggests to me that, although there were times when he was deeply distressed for others, he had an inner strength and calm which came from his single-mindedness.

Maybe it helps us as we think about peace. The struggle for peace is won and lost, not in the outside world, but in the world within each one of us. It's the struggle to see ourselves as we really are, not only to ourselves but to God; and then to realise that he accepts us and surrounds us with his love. It's when we come to terms with ourselves, and offer what we are to God, that the seed of 'peace' is established.

"Peace be with you." That's what you said, Lord.
"My peace I give to you." That too, Lord.
And yet at times it seems so illusive. So hard to find.
And when it's in my grasp, and I hold on tight,
it disappears.
Then I look at the world.
All I see is struggle. Conflict.
People at war with each other, killing for peace. Or so they say.
Although how one can make the other I can't work out.
At war with the world.
Exploiting, destroying your creation, for a quick profit.
At war with themselves.
Anxious, fearful, dislocated.
Without hope or purpose. Lonely.
Living from one crisis to the next.

Where **is** *your peace, Lord?*
What are you trying to tell me?
When Jesus offered his peace
he was facing the cross. Head on.
And it wasn't just words.
He could talk of peace, while he felt the pain,
because he was at peace.

At peace with you
because he knew he was doing your will.
At peace with others
because nothing they did to him could break his love for them.
At peace with himself
because he was true to himself.
And as I identify with him, Lord,
as I discover the strength of your love,
as I come to terms with what I am
and know that I am still accepted, the peace is there.
I can drop my defences.
I pray for all who need your peace today.
Help me to reach out with your healing.
Not just medicine but healing.
Building a community, relationships.
Building your kingdom.
Making peace, in your name.

Hanging on

Luke 9:51-62

I WAS WATCHING the London Marathon on television. It's a great occasion, with thousands of runners. Amateur and professional, men and women of all ages train for months. Then they run in a 26-mile race through London. Of all the runners only about 1,000 drop out, the rest complete the course.

Several of the serious athletes talked about something they called the 'pain barrier'. They each said that the first 15 or 16 miles went well. They found a rhythm of breathing and running which carried them along but then, quite suddenly, it all disappeared. They felt distressed. Their breath became irregular, their legs went weak, the rhythm vanished, and all they knew was a great pain right through their bodies. No matter how hard they trained, it always happened. When it does, you have to grit your teeth, summon up all your determination and courage, and just hang on. Some runners give up at that point, but if you keep going, you eventually pass through the pain barrier. You find that the rhythm and strength return, the pain ebbs, and you are running competently again. It takes courage to hold on, but it's the only way forward.

It's a long time ago, but I remember a similar thing when I trained in a commando course in the Royal Navy. Faced with tough physical demands in the rope-crossing of small rivers, climbing walls in full kit, crawling through mud and barbed wire, utter exhaustion brought you near to tears of frustration. A few dropped out, but if you crawled on, even cursing the whole idea as you went, you eventually got through. And it felt great!

We all meet pain barriers of one sort or another, and we don't need to be athletes to understand them. There are times when a relationship goes wrong or a serious obstacle gets in our way, and all we feel is pain. Being a Christian doesn't necessarily ease the pain, and certainly doesn't make the problem disappear. (However much the athlete trains he always has to cope with the pain barrier.) We can pray for a miracle, Christians often do. Sometimes miracles happen, but my Christian experience shows that more often we just have to face the moment as it comes. We have to find that extra bit of strength from our prayer, scrape that extra bit of courage from the faith that God knows and cares, and hang on to the encouragement of friends around. Yes, I know we have to put it into the Lord's hands, but even then we have to take some responsibility ourselves. That's the hard part.

Yet, however hard the road, however long it takes, there comes a point where we break through our personal pain barrier onto the smoother road ahead. The pain recedes, the rhythm returns, and we're running again. And the real miracle is not that something spectacular happened, but that we found the courage and strength to keep going, to hang on. Then we can look back and find that the Lord was with us, even when we felt most lonely and vulnerable. Especially then. The important thing is to keep moving ahead.

"No one who puts his hand to the plough," said Jesus, "and looks back is fit for service in the kingdom of God" (Luke 9:62).

Old Homestead, New Zealand

It all seemed fine, Lord.
Walking along, not a care in the world, everything going right.
I was even remembering to say the occasional thank you to you,
when it changed.
The sun clouded over. A cold wind blew out of nowhere.
The first drops of rain splattered down
hitting the warm, dry earth of my path with a finality
that said the weather's changed. I shivered.

Lord, when things go wrong help me to remember the good times.
When my life with you, and my fellow Christians,
hits rock bottom and I find it hard to take,
stay with me.
*No, that's wrong, Lord. You **are** with me,*
I know it.
Just help me to feel it.
Not just the theory, but the experience.
When I'm disappointed
and hurt by outside events,
by the way others behave,
when I'm honest enough to look at myself
and admit that the fault often lies inside me,
then let me feel you near.
And when the pain is bad,
when the sheer effort of keeping my feet
moving along your road,
when the scenic route through the mountains
–AA recommended –
turns into the rocky path of a small Calvary,
give me the strength to go on.

It would be easy, sometimes, to give up.
To drop out at the roadside, a casualty.
A great future behind me.
I'm not sure, at times, why I do go on, until,
when I get out onto the other side of the pain,
and warm myself again in your sunshine,
I know.
You were with me. Are with me.
Lord, I pray for those
in the middle of their pain barrier today.

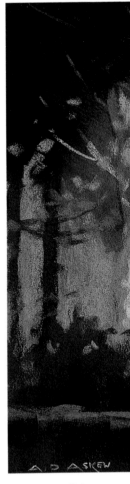

Filtered sunlight

46

*Trying to stay on the road, putting everything they've got
into the effort of getting through to the night.
Through the cloud of uncertainty,
may they be sure of your love.
In the loneliness,
may they feel your arm slipped through theirs.
In the darkness of depression,
may they hold on to the promise of your light.*

*Help us, Lord,
Just to keep moving.*

Pastel

When things go wrong

Luke 22:31-34

TWO LETTERS from different African countries reflect recent violence. The first reports that a leprosy centre '... had been attacked several times by guerrillas. Five leprosy patients lost their lives in the shooting and two health workers died from a mine on the road ... the centre has been closed and evacuated ... This is a land of suffering and death...'

The second reports, 'Around the hospital, where the actual war was fought, four leprosy sufferers were shot dead, clergy and deacons were killed. It is indeed terrible here. Most of the patients who were in hiding have returned. Their property is burnt and looted ... I also fled to escape ... My brother was shot dead and burnt in his house. My house and property was destroyed too...'

My mind was drawn recently to the book of Daniel – not one of my favourites. Do you remember Shadrach, Meshach and Abednego (the trouble I had with those names as a child, and even worse with King Nebuchadnezzar) and their refusal to deny their God? The King threatens them with fire but they affirm their faith in a God who is able to rescue them. And then comes a mind-catching phrase: "but even if he does not ... still we will not serve your gods" (Daniel 3:18).

To begin with it's an honest acknowledgement of the fact that things don't always go right for God's people. That's pretty self-evident to anyone who looks at the world realistically, although I do meet blinkered Christians who seem to imply that if only we'd get right with the Lord – as individuals and as nations – everything in life would be fine! It just doesn't happen that way. And it's not always our fault – don't get hung up searching for personal guilt when things go wrong, that's just inhibiting. Faith isn't an all-risks insurance policy. (On second thoughts: maybe it is. Insurance doesn't prevent accidents but it gives you a secure base from which to face the consequences.) It isn't a cure-all. If it were, if faith prevented the pain and the problems, the queues outside the church buildings would be enormous. Sometimes faith and pain go together, and it's the unrighteous who have it good.

"But even if he doesn't ..." It's also a courageous statement of faith in God's purposes. Not necessarily accepting that whatever hits us comes straight from God – I'm wary of these over-simplifications of why calamities happen – but faith in the way he can and does use events to shape and refine us. A faith which springs from the experience of God-with-us through many crises. Ed. Ingebretsen, an American Jesuit poet, writes:

... your violence, Lord, opens more worlds than closes;
... we are stones, sons of black rock;
crush the veins, grind, hew, hone.
Free the waiting diamond.

... we are steel, straighten, stretch, fine –
melt us, shape, thin us like strong wires.
we are seed, dry, desiccated –
rain us, green us as once we were:
The harvest remembers not the cut.

He proclaims faith in his continuing love and concern, however hot the fire. Rescue may come or not; faith shows its strength in accepting, at times, God's non-intervention. It's not a glib, easy acceptance. It takes courage simply to pray 'but not my will' and mean it!

City Flats, Kowloon

Lord, that's the way I'd like to live.
Fearless, honest.
Looking life straight in the eye whatever comes.
Facing the reality of the world with your courage.
Not flinching at the furnace.
Staying faithful to you.
Hoping for rescue, but standing up anyway. Upright, dependable.
Even when the consequences are clear to see. And frightening.
Finding the strength to stand firm.
Knowing that you are here, through good and bad.

The trouble is,
looking at me, you'd never believe it.
Because try as I may
the picture never looks like that.
However much I struggle with the outline
the details don't fill in the way they should.
I look at the furnace, feel the heat,
and the sweat breaks out.
Not the hot sweat of commitment.
The cold sweat of fear.
And when I think about it
afterwards,
when I recognise the denial,
I can't look myself in the eye.
I'm ashamed.

Lift my head up, Lord,
so that as I look into your eyes
my shame evaporates
in the warmth of your love.
Give me the courage to start again.
And help me to see
that your love comes in many disguises.
Help me to grasp that truth,
more real than reality.
Teach me, teach all your children,
to feel your love,
not only in the gentle whispers of life,
but in the black boiling storm clouds
which threaten us with crisis.

Show us its presence
not only in birth-joy
but in the death of the seed.
Resurrection at the door of the tomb.

And, somehow, Lord,
give me the courage
to welcome your love
in all its disguises.

Sussex Village

Travelling slowly

Psalm 103:1-11

THE BEST travel books, the ones full of discovery and interest, are written by people who travel slowly. It takes time to see, to think, to experience and then to understand. Not the blast of jet engines and the ten-countries-in-eight-days syndrome, but the slower, contemplative journeys. I'm not joining the fashion which derides rapid travel altogether. It's useful, and I wonder how else one would keep up with rapid changes today, but the trouble is that the speed of travel conditions us to expect equal speed in other affairs. I notice how much more often we ask "When do we arrive?" than "What can I see on the way?"

But this same concern for speed affects our inward journey, too. Just as we fuss over a few hours' delay at an airport, so we demand instant results in our inner exploration. We look at ourselves (at least, some of us do. I'm still surprised at the number of folk who don't look inwards to discover what is there) and, disappointed by what we see, we long for change. Dissatisfied, we get angry with ourselves, and with our inability to respond rapidly. Often it hides under a cloak of anger towards others. "Why doesn't she change?" often masks anger at our own difficulties in facing change. And, underneath, this anger creates tension, and we punish ourselves without mercy. The desert through which we travel is not out there but, as a poet wrote, 'squeezed in the tube-train next to you, the desert is in the heart of your brother.' And in your own.

I came across a writer the other day who said that after years of deep self-criticism he had learnt that '...we must be patient with ourselves, just as God is infinitely patient with us.' It's worth repeating that to love our neighbours as ourselves implies the pre-condition that we love ourselves. Not by pampering ourselves, or by demanding more that we are entitled to – that is spoiling ourselves as indulgent parents spoil their children – but in facing honestly what we are and coming to terms with it. Then, with God's help, going about the job of reconstruction with the same patience towards ourselves that God has with us.

Meeting people who are unhappy with external problems, or with their inner response, I realise that a phrase I use often is 'Give it time'. It's not always appreciated, but patience is more constructive than anger and is a necessary part of positive Christian living. An understanding and relaxed acceptance of oneself is a first step towards the wholeness which Kalahari bushmen call 'walking again with the moon and the stars'. It's a balanced, well-navigated way of life which is the Biblical *shalom* – the God-created harmony of life with the Lord, with our fellows, with work and nature, and with ourselves. That is the peace that transcends all understanding.

Thank you for your patience, Lord.
For your understanding
of my doubts, and errors and weaknesses.
Thank you for coming to me,
not in a blinding flash of retribution, but in love.
It's good to know I'm in your hands.

I don't understand it fully, Lord –
Oh! Let me be honest, I don't understand it at all –
your patience.
'A thousand years in your sight ...'
Yes, I know you're not limited to time,
like me and yet ...
yet – am I limited to time?
Haven't you invited me to share in your kingdom?
Haven't you planted eternity in my heart?
Lord, maybe that's where your patience comes from.
From the knowledge that you have time.
All the time in the world. And beyond.
But more, your patience comes from love.
The willingness to pick me up, and start again
every time I fall.

It makes me think, Lord,
if you have all this patience with me,
shouldn't I have patience too?
With myself –
not just to indulge myself,
not to gloss over the person I am,
but to do what you do –
pick up the pieces of my life and start again.
Without resentment, without building up that anger against myself
which leaves me exhausted,
and helpless, and full of guilt.
Knowing that time is in your hands, and so am I.
To accept myself as you accept me.
Knowing all the faults, but seeing
with the eyes of love and forgiveness.
And, knowing that you do that for me,
help me to do it,
not only for myself
but for others.

You are still there, with your forgiveness.

Guernsey Beach

Pastel

If only...

1 John 4:13-19

I HOPE I don't sound chauvinistic when I say I'm always happy to be in England at Easter. It's simply that in this part of the world, Easter and Spring come together, and the experience of death and new life is underlined beautifully in the new leaf, and the audacious flowering of spring blossom. Brilliant colour springing from the dark earth. And though it comes suddenly, breathtakingly, it is the result of a process going on through the winter, unseen but powerful, quietly working away in the dark and cold.

Over Easter I was thinking about Judas's betrayal of Jesus, and doing a bit of 'if only ...'. Judas, slowly realising the enormity of his actions, reaching that point of darkness where guilt and horror and fear spill over into consciousness, rushes out and hangs himself. He threw away more that the 30 pieces of silver – he threw away his life. If only ... he had waited. Because Judas died at the dawn of forgiveness. He died while Jesus was on his way to the cross, on the way to that greatest act of reconciliation which brings us, sinful as we are, back into fellowship with God. And which, surely, could have done the same for Judas! One can only think that Judas (if he articulated his fears in those lost and last few minutes) believed that there was no hope for him, because he had denied everything of real value. But so did Peter, and there was forgiveness for him – Jesus forgave and restored. Thomas refused to believe – Jesus made a special point of meeting his need. Would he not have done the same for Judas?

There's something here for each one of us. I've known people in depression: full of remorse and guilt, unable to see light or hope, seeing only their own unworthiness. I've known others, just unable to believe that Christ's love is for them, because they don't merit it. All right, none of us is worthy, but that's not the criterion. Love isn't created by the 'niceness' or 'worthiness' of our natures. The truth is, thank God, that love springs from the nature of the one who loves, that is, from God. It is because God is love that we are loved and 'In this way, love is made complete among us so that we may have confidence on the day of judgement ...' (1 John 4:17). Read the rest yourself.

And that love, incarnate in Jesus, brought forgiveness for all who will take it – Judas, or me – and that is our confidence and our hope. If only Judas had waited what a witness he would have made. Think of Paul, the killer of Christians, the enemy of Christ, and yet later exulting, "Christ lives in me." I wonder what the Gospel according to Judas could have been? Perhaps it would have begun, 'Hold on to hope, love is alive, strong, and flowering anew above the dark earth. Hallelujah.'

Lord, I realise that what I see of your love
is only the beginning.
One drop from the whole ocean.
And, like the sea, moving, surging.
All embracing.
Seeking to surround me, not to overwhelm, to drown,
but to hold me, buoy me up.
A love with room to spare.
No rejections.
No high tidemark of rubbish,
pushed up and thrown aside.

I wish Judas could have known that.
I wish that somehow
in his own agony in the garden,
so different, Lord, from yours,
so like mine,
he could have reached out from the depths of his despair
and felt your hand.
There's nothing I can do about that.
I leave it with you, Lord,
as I leave so much.
You've got strong hands.

But one thing, Lord.
Judas stays in my thoughts
and, in a strange way,
comforts me.
Because I know beyond doubt
that when I'm nearly overwhelmed
by my own betrayals,
it isn't you who puts space between us.
It's me.
You are still there,
with your forgiveness.
As you forgave Peter,
and Thomas, and Paul,
so you forgive me.
And accept me, as you accepted them.
Thank you seems so small a word,
but it's all I've got.

Thank you for differences

Genesis 1:26-31

USING THE OFFICE photocopier the other day, I watched perfect copies of a letter being churned out, one every two seconds. I thought: 'If only I could put one of our workers in there'. Choose the best and out would come dozens of perfect replicas. No more staffing problems. An attractive idea until I remembered a phrase of John Taylor's, about 'Xerox-people' – the way the world tries to regiment us, tries to mould us to a blank uniformity of image – and I didn't like the idea any more.

Newspaper and television advertising give us the perfect image of the consumer. We must all use a certain margarine and a particular soap powder. Everyone who aspires to be someone uses Dior perfume, and holidays in the Caribbean. What, all at once? Maybe the perfume keeps us smelling fresh while our slim bodies (thank you, margarine) bask in the Caribbean sun on our whiter-than-white towels (thank you, soap powder)? A whole industry geared to make man in the image of man. No, it's not such a good idea, to be turned into clones of each other.

There's a paradox, though. We are all the same, in the way we're made, in our basic needs and hopes. Yet we are all different, in personality, in aptitudes and interests, and it's the differences which make you you, and me me. The same yet different, and interdependent, like twigs on a tree. And while we value our togetherness as human beings we need to respect and accept the individuality which makes our personalities. These are the differences which enrich the human family. Some folk take the conformity idea further, and try to make God in their own image, trying to force him into the mould of their own particular beliefs and limiting the work of the Spirit to their own special tramlines. Setting boundaries to the way he can act. I sometimes think God must find it difficult to believe in our God!

The great thing is that he doesn't do the same with us. Experience shows me that God doesn't expect us all to do things in the same way. He respects our personalities, even to the point of giving us the freedom to reject him, if we want to. And when we do try to live for him, even then he respects our individuality. I wish more Christians would grasp this. If God loves our individuality, can't we? We generate so much tension inside ourselves by trying to conform to self-imposed ideas of behaviour – a religiousness, really. And the best unasked-for-advice I can give is 'be yourself' although it goes without saying I mean 'in Christ'. If you try to be like anyone else, as a friend said to me recently, the Lord will say: "No thanks, I already have one like that."

Lord, I've seen the looks.
The warm summer day when I turned up at church
in a bush shirt. No tie. No jacket.
No, not everyone's looks.
But enough to make me wonder.
The criticism, thinly disguised as a joke.
I thought it was the worship that mattered
but apparently it's being in step. Conforming.
Doing things the same way everyone else does.
It's not just your church, Lord.
It's just that your church
seems to have taken its lead from the world.
Government, big business, the organisers.
The computer isn't programmed to cope with individuality.
(We mustn't blame the computer. It's programmed by people!)
We must be all the same.
The same mould, the straightjacket of uniformity.

Thank you for all that make us different, Lord.
For the variety of your world.
I suppose creation could have been easier
if you'd only chosen one green,
but when I stand in a field and absorb the landscape
there must be a hundred greens, all different.
Light and dark, warm and cold, intense and pale.
That's the beauty, the joy.
It would be insane to try to repaint them all the same.
And yet I see folk doing just that to each other.
To themselves.

Lord, forgive us for rejecting the diversity of your world,
its wonder, its change.
For denying the marvellous mosaic of human personality.
For loving ourselves so little that we box ourselves in
with rules that you've never made.
Help us to see that in Christ we are free.
Free. Not to trample on the freedom of others,
but free to be ourselves.
Free to laugh. Free to live.
Free, within the endless bounds of love, to grow.
Free to reflect your image, in our diversity.

You lead me out into the wide
open spaces of your freedom.

After the Shower

Watercolour

Space for others

Galatians 5:13-18

IN LESOTHO, I was standing in the sun looking out over a wide green plain. Across it, a few small villages strung like beads along a red thread of dirt road, a group of horsemen cantering towards the far blue hills. A bird hovered, watchful, holding itself in balance with slight movements of wing. It was all openness, clarity, light, space. Room for the mind to expand, space for living. A friend to whom I'd been talking had described human relationships as 'creating space for others'. It's a good starting point.

"I am come," said Jesus, "that you may have life, and have it to the full" (John 10:10). Full life demands space, mental as well as physical, and we're quick to create the space we need for ourselves. An elbow poaching on the armrest as I settle down to another long flight from London, guarding our territory and authority to preserve the space we need to act as we want to. But what about other people's need of space? As we find the space to put our feet down, do we trespass on that of our neighbours? Do our relationships create space for them?

I remember the paternal/maternal attitudes I've seen some in missionaries who always 'know best' what their people need, and who are really meeting their own needs by pushing people around 'for their own good'. Acting out the role of the benefactor, rather than creating the space in which people can learn to develop their own lives. Maybe it's a particular danger for Christians, as we seek to share our experience of God's love in Jesus Christ, to try to impose on other people the blessings we have found. But you can't impose freedom. The fullness of life that Jesus offers is offered with the right to refuse it. That's part of his loving concern for personality, and it's part of this creating of space for others I'm thinking about. It's hard to watch people turn their backs on him (it's hard for him!), but if the Lord allows people the space they need, then it has to be good enough for us. It's important in all our relationships with our co-workers, our friends (not always identical), even – perhaps especially – within marriage. Acknowledging in the closest relationships the freedom of partners to have personalities of their own, not imposed by obligation or domination.

And I'm sad when I see people so repressed by their taboos and narrow ideas of what God expects of them, that they deny themselves the space they need to open their minds wide to the liberation Christ brings. "I am come that you may have life," not confined to a little box, however pretty the wrapping paper, but in a wide open plain, creating space for the spirit to walk, to run, to fly.

Lord, I'm quick to stake my claim to territory.
To elbow people aside and tell them "This is mine".
To create and hold my own small kingdom against all comers.
I need space,
and I get all uptight when I feel hemmed in;
when people, even friends, intrude across my frontiers,
telling me what to do, and how to do it.
I need to work things out for myself if I'm to grow.

Forgive me, Lord, that I don't do for others
what I want them to do for me.
Because, in my arrogance
- although I don't usually call it that,
I call it helpfulness -
I push myself forward into other people's lives.
It's hard to find the balance, Lord, the sensitivity.
Some folk are crying out,
silently, for help.
Others just want to be left alone.
Help me to feel the difference.
Help me to look for marks of welcome
before I gatecrash with the small gift of my advice.
Give me the grace to stand back,
to keep my shadow out of their light.

But when I'm ready
- your graciousness again -
you lead me out
into the wide open spaces of your freedom.
And I find that I can stretch, and walk, and run
in your great plains of liberty,
kicking my heels in joy,
all restraints gone,
except the welcome yoke of your love.
And I can grow.

Welsh Farmhouse

The freedom road

Luke 7:18-23

JOHN BAPTIST is an intriguing figure: disturbing, ascetic, blowing in from the wilderness like a scorching wind. Free, aggressive, challenging establishment and individual with his conviction of the coming Messiah; confronting them with the need radically to reshape their lives and attitudes. And confirmation came with Jesus. "This is the one," said John. Then – prison. John is seized. A man used to life in the desert, walking the mountains at will, John is now confined. Doubts grow, and John sends messengers to Jesus. From preaching "This is the one", he now asks, "Are you the one?" Jesus doesn't give a straight answer. Why couldn't Jesus simply have said "Yes"? There's still a good deal of preaching around which puts Jesus up as the one who answers all our questions and solves all our problems. Well he is, ultimately, but not in the sense of giving instant ready-made solutions. Many folk would like that – press the prayer-button and the printout gives detailed instructions telling us exactly what to think, say and do.

There are Christian groups who try to organise life in that way, both for themselves and their followers. It seems to me, though, that the more detailed the instructions get, the more restrictive they are, and the more man-made they appear, rather than God-given. The Christian faith is about freedom – sometimes joyful freedom, sometimes a frightening freedom. There's the road ahead, sometimes clear, sometimes ill-defined. At moments the journey may seem like an organised group tour, but more often it's a pilgrimage, an exploration into little-known territory. And Jesus' promise to be with us always is not so much as a tour guide but as the strength which helps us face up to the uncertainty of the road. We are not provided with tailor-made answers, but with a better set of questions. When Peter asked how many times he should forgive a brother who made life hard for him, he was hoping for clear limits. Jesus told him the question was wrong. The answer is love, not mathematics. "How many times do you want God to forgive you, Peter?" It's harder, but there's no freedom in following detailed instructions, only a moving back towards slavery.

Going back to John Baptist, I believe Jesus is saying, "Look, John. You know who I am already. Just look at what I'm doing, take hold of the facts you have, put them together." Faith is the essence. Push-button answers to our problems would destroy faith, not strengthen it. It is the exercise of trust which deepens faith, the willingness to move forward, not always knowing what will happen, but facing uncertainty in the light and security of his strength and love.

Lord, sometimes your approach to things
is a bit disconcerting.
You invite me to follow you,
ask me to commit my life to you,
and then, when I ask for the rule book
there doesn't seem to be one.
It's breathtaking, the freedom you offer me.
Wonderful, and frightening.
You offer to share your work with me,
and leave so much of it for me to get on with.
I struggle with my own faith, Lord, and yet here you are
showing so much more faith in me, in spite of all my failures.
I'm impressed. I'm frightened too.
There's so much freedom, maybe I'll get lost.

I'd like the comfort of a rule book. I'd know exactly where I was.
It would be easier living that way,
being able to tick off the do's and don'ts.
Yet would it?
I've lived by rules. I wore a uniform, in earlier days.
I had my life regulated exactly, minutely, by officers in gold braid.
And if I remember rightly, honestly,
I spent a lot of time carrying out the letter, and ignoring the spirit.
Trying to see how nearly I could break the rules
without being caught.
Doing only the minimum to keep out of trouble.

Lord, it's not worthy of your service, to box it in with rules.
I thank you for your Word.
And I acknowledge, with joy,
that however much I try to make its words conform to my image,
it escapes me.
The rules I make melt away in the warmth of your love.

Lord, give me the courage to live in your freedom.
Help me to think for myself.
To strike out into the unknown
confident that though I don't know the way, you do.
And when I'm feeling unsure,
and insecure in my first steps,
let me feel your hand there to support me.

So much to do

John 15:1-10

I WAS READING an article the other day by the French Christian writer, Michel Quoist, on having too much to do. He writes of the way we often feel that:

we are doing only one-tenth of what we can see we should be doing;

we are doing only one-hundredth of what we could do if only ...

we are doing only one-thousandth of what we would like to do ...

and of the difficulty most of us have in coming to terms with our limitations. We all know the feeling. We get anxious and frustrated – so much to do, so little time and energy to do it. Other people aren't doing what we feel should be done, or are doing it differently, or doing things we think are wrong. And that leads to more anxiety and frustration.

Of course, we can check our priorities and make sure we're doing the most important things. (Not necessarily the ones we enjoy doing most!) We can look at our efficiency and try not to waste time or energy. But even when we've done all that, there is still more than we can do.

One question – if you really don't have time to do something, what makes you think God wants *you* to do it? Sit back and think about that one. Don't we sometimes overstretch ourselves because we can't admit that we are near our limits, because we can't say, 'no.' (Actually, our colleagues usually know when we're at our limit before we do, although they often put up with our tenseness – and worse – without saying anything.)

Too often we act as though we were alone. Jesus said, "I am the vine; you are the branches" (John 15:5). Note the plural "branches". There are many branches, not just one. My job is just part of the whole, and if I truly can't cope with all I'm trying to do, maybe I'm trying to do the job of other branches as well as my own. I find it very challenging that Jesus' words about the vine run on to a statement about his love for us, and our need to dwell in his love (John 15:10). It suggests to me that it's not so much the amount we do – ruling out any encouragement to laziness or irresponsibility – as the quality of what we do. The person who tries frantically to do more and more, and to make other people do things his way is in danger of losing love in the process – love for people, and their love for him. Fruitfulness comes more from a loving spirit than a domineering one; more from the humility of accepting one's limitations than from a frenetic battle to squeeze 48 hours into 24.

Lord, when I think about it,
I reckon I sometimes come to you to show you how much I'm doing.
To encourage you to tell me
what a hardworking, good and faithful servant I really am.
I sometimes wonder how you'd get on without me!
Forgive my pride, Lord.
Forgive me for believing there are no limits to what I can do.
Forgive me for trying to do so much for you that I do most of it badly.
Forgive my arrogance that says if I don't do it
it'll never get done at all.
Sometimes it does seem like that.
But when I look at it coolly – help me to do that, Lord,
I reckon your kingdom needs as many cool heads
as it needs warm hearts –
I'm really saying that you couldn't do it, if I weren't here.
That if I weren't rushing around like a juggler
with 20 plates in the air all at once,
your kingdom would collapse.

Lord, forgive me for telling myself that I'm the vine,
and all the branches as well.
Help me to acknowledge that you are in control,
and that I'm just one of the branches. Just one.
I've seen vines, Lord. And although I'm no winegrower
I know the branches have to be pruned.
And if one tries to take over it gets cut back.
Give me the humility to see that the more I try to do
the more I'm shutting other people out.
Letting them think they're not needed.
Not encouraging them, because it's all better done my way.

And when my energy is draining away
like water down the whirlpool of my own frantic busyness,
slow me down.
Gently. Lovingly.
Help me relax in you.
Help me to understand that your kingdom is on its way
even when I can't take on any more.
And help me to realise
that when there seems to be no one else around
to do all that needs doing,
you are.

Autumn Trees

Thank you for being the
strong ground in which
I sow my life.

Watercolour

No short cuts

1 John 1:1-4

HERE ARE the words of a Christian writer I came across the other day: 'God, to me, is a verb not a noun'. Of course God *is,* unchangeable, eternal, but we know him through his active presence with us. God is at work, not only in creation, but in sustaining and rescuing that creation. John's Gospel echoes this: '... and all that came to be was alive with his life' (John 1:3 NEB), and the rest of the Good News shows us God at work in the world – seeking, healing, loving, reconciling. God continually at work as he draws us closer. God, an active, living presence, his life made visible and experiential in and through Jesus Christ.

It's easy, at this point, to fall into the trap of Western activism, the temptation always to be doing in response to any situation. "What are you doing about it?" is one of our most common questions, and anyone who replies: "I'm waiting to see how it develops", is immediately suspect. If God is active, then surely we must be active too. But if our activity is to be effective it must be rooted in God, and rooting takes time. The tree produces its branches, buds, leaves, flowers and fruit only from the strength of a hidden but stable root system. To work for God we must know him and feed on him, so that our activity is his activity. Knowing God liberates us from "The dark little dungeon of my own ego", as Malcolm Muggeridge puts it, and leads us into the freedom of acting within God's will and not our own, and with the honesty not to equate the two without great care.

There's one more danger point. We want to share our experience – we feel we must share it – whether it be the experience of the freedom Christ brings, or our professional expertise as doctors, nurses, administrators, whatever. We rush in, expecting our knowledge and advice to be swallowed whole (after all, we know what we are doing, while these folk ...?). And when the recipients of our offers are sceptical, or resistant, or plain uninterested, we get disillusioned.

Recent experience in South East Asia has helped my understanding. On an earlier visit, five years ago, in some areas the Mission's workers faced real conflict and frustration. In one place, we seriously considered pulling out, but we didn't. Today, what a difference. I'm not saying there are no frustrations anymore (I wouldn't dare) but there is an acceptance of our presence and work, and a new atmosphere in which things can get done. Thinking about it, I believe that in that area we have now earned the right to speak, to teach. As a result of patiently living, learning, working and caring, people can discern 'the life made visible'; can experience the verb of service, and not just the noun of advice. We have earned the right to speak. Each one of us, whatever the situation, has to earn that right for himself.

It's not given to us just because we've crossed a political border, or because of our paper qualifications. We need those as credentials to cross borders or to begin work, but our right to speak, to be taken seriously by the people we serve, comes through the slow building of friendship, relationship and confidence. That can't be hurried and when, given time, we get there, the things we want to do and teach may be modified by the learning along the road.

There are no short cuts, except to disappointment, and there is no Calvary bypass.

Changing Moods

Watercolour

Thank you for all you do for me, Lord. And for all you do
for this restless world I live in.
For the life you create and sustain.
For your love which holds and feeds me, and gives me strength.
For your activity underlying the universe,
gradually, patiently, working out your purposes
– in spite of all I do to help!

And thank you for what you are,
not just for what you do.
Thank you
for being the strong ground in which I
sow my life,
the sure goodness in which all good
is rooted,
and the love from which all love
is harvested.

Lord, there's a time for work
and there's a time for waiting,
a time to let your love soak in.
Sinking into the hot dry earth
of my being.
Cool, refreshing, renewing.
The trouble lies with me, Lord.
The easy way I convince myself
that if I'm not moving
everything stops.
The way I substitute action for devotion,
and hide from your view behind a dust
cloud of doing.
Doing, always doing,
in a restless fever of activity,
fingers plucking
at the bed sheets of being
yet never straightening them out.

But don't I have to share your love,
share it with others?
And isn't the only way
– you see, I'm not giving in easily, Lord –
to do something?

Morning Light, Norway

Then another question hits me
- you punch low, sometimes, Lord.
If I don't have time for you,
no time to be,
no time for just you and me in the quietness,
if I don't open myself to your love
unhurried, uncluttered,
then what do I have to share?

Watercolour

Untie the knots

Matthew 21:1-9

IN THE DAYS of the Cultural Revolution it was easy to wonder if the Christian faith would survive in the People's Republic of China. Almost all Church buildings were closed, or used for other purposes. Christians were 're-educated' and dispersed. Yet out of China today comes increasing evidence of Christian survival, and of growth. Thank God for resurrection, renewal, new life. A report describes a middle-aged woman evangelist in China. Somehow she has the freedom to move around, sharing her faith and joy with small communities of believers. Her witness and teaching add to their numbers, and there are many more like her, unnamed and unknown to us.

She calls herself 'the Lord's donkey' – a humble believer carrying the Lord around with her wherever she goes. It's a great symbol. It suggests the patient willingness to bear a burden, to be used as God wants to use us, uncomplaining. I suspect too, that he could use far more donkeys in his work, and far fewer of the prancing, temperamental racehorses many us seem to be.

Another point. When Jesus sent his disciples to get the donkey he was to ride into Jerusalem, it was 'tied up'. Only when it was untied, liberated, was it useful. How 'tied up' are you, in busyness, in your own affairs? Or are you so tied up emotionally or spiritually that you need the Lord to slice through the knots before he can use you? There's a danger in the donkey image, though – of seeing ourselves simply as burden bearers. It's easy to think that the weight is all on our shoulders, almost as though the Lord were content to sit on our backs and allow us to do all the work. From there it's not far to feeling indispensable and 'the one thing we don't need is indispensable people'. To put the picture straight, let me share a parable I read recently, and which I now modify a bit.

Life, said the teacher, is like a mountain. A man climbs with effort, sometimes with joy, sometimes in a storm. Climbing higher, he looks back and sees two sets of footprints in the snow – his and the Lord's. Looking more carefully, he sees patches of difficult climbing with only one set of footprints visible. "Hey, Lord," he says, "I thought you promised to be with me, always?" "That's right," answers the Lord. "The places where you see only one set of footprints are the times I carried you." Just as Jesus 'carried' the bewildered disciples on the road to Emmaus without their recognising him, supporting them through grief, pain and tiredness, so he supports you and me, and brings us out into the joy again. Really it's not an either/or choice; it's both being the donkey and the companion, all at the same time.

Sometimes I feel like a donkey, Lord.
Overburdened. Not very bright. Taken for granted.
There's always room on my back
for one more burden. So people think.
Sometimes they dangle a carrot in front of me,
to encourage me to do more.
Sometimes they show me a stick.
And still I go plodding on.

When I think about it, that's often the way I treat people.
Unthinking. Unfeeling. Just assuming they're there.
But before I get too sorry for myself
I need to remember your donkey.
Tied up, doing nothing. Until your call came.
It's good to be needed,
to know that my efforts aren't all wasted.
That you can untie my knots, free me, use me.
And what use! God's son, sitting on my back.
Forgive me, Lord, for the times when I see that as a burden,
instead of a glorious privilege.
Forgive me for wishing you'd get on with things without my help,
and leave me quietly chewing the hay.
Yet I'm glad you need me.
I need the boost it gives to my self-esteem, knowing that.
I hope it's not just ego, Lord.
But if I'm to respect others, love others, as myself,
I need to see myself the same way.

There are limits though. The donkey can only do so much.
There came a time, Lord,
just a few days after the donkey ride,
when it wasn't the donkey taking the strain.
It was you, carrying the weight. On the cross.
Taking the burden of a world gone wrong.
Taking responsibility for all its mistakes –
shall we stop treading delicately
and call it sin, Lord, our sin, my sin?
Carrying it all, carrying me,
to the gates of your Kingdom.

You needed the donkey, Lord, just for a time.
I need you. Always.

Labels

Romans 8:14-18

SOME TIME AGO, a group of people hired a bus to do the overland journey from London to New Delhi. It was an economy trip, with much camping out and cooking. Tinned food was carried in the luggage compartments beneath the bus. In fording rivers the tins were submerged and many of the food labels floated loose. One traveller said that eating became an adventure. They would buy meat on the way, cook it, and then open some tins to go with it. They never knew whether they'd get peas, or apricots, or sweet rice pudding.

Labels help, when it comes to food or other consumer goods, but not with people. It's so easy to label. Two historical social debates come to mind: one over strikes in the motor industry, the other over the far more important issue of nuclear weapons. Labels are attached to people with little thought, but great emotion. It was either 'Industrial managers are inhuman' or 'Union leaders are greedy'. In the other dispute it was either 'Nuclear disarmers are Communists' or 'Supporters of nuclear deterrence are warmongers'. Everyone docketed and classified. It's neat, reassuring. You know where you stand. Christians do it, Lord forgive us. Evangelical or Liberal. Mostly, it's a snap judgement, a prejudice, based on transmitted custom within our particular group, and on the pictures we hold in our minds. Yet people are not stereotypes. We don't fall off the end of an assembly line, all neatly programmed to react in the same way. People are different, and similar only in their diversity – in the mixture of good and bad, in the richness of experience to which we are continually adding from birth. You and I realise we are made up that way, and we hope that others will allow us the freedom to be what we are. Can't we do the same for them? Can't we accept people unlabelled?

Another problem is that labels can restrict our own development. Our traditional piety sometimes makes us less than fully human. We curb our ability to enjoy life, or feel pain, because we feel we must conform to an expected role, to labels we stick on ourselves. Yet the most important thing is not that we can recognise others, labelled or not, nor that they acknowledge our labels, but rather that God recognises us. And the thing he recognises is love, not labels. That's what he identifies with. Not the classification by which we proclaim our separateness from others, and certainly not the critical labels we apply to them, but the caring which shows our identification with them. What we claim to be is not as important as the presence of Christ in our lives. That's what leads God to call us his children. 'Because those who are led (not labelled!) by the Spirit are sons (and daughters) of God' (Romans 8:14).

*They put labels on **you**, Lord.*
Friend of sinners, Sabbath breaker.
Disturber of the peace.
They put all their fear and anger,
all their hate, into their labels.
It was easier to label than to listen.
Easier to condemn than to have their world altered,
their customs questioned.
Easier to keep the blinkers on than face the light,
the discomfort of truth,
Your truth. Living truth.

They even nailed a label to your cross.
Just above the thorns of a bloody crown.
King of the Jews, it said.
Label. Laugh. Turn away. Forget.

Is that what I do, Lord?
The mockery of quick judgement
that takes fear as evidence,
prejudice as reason.
That shoots on sight
and leaves the bleeding body of truth
dead in a ditch.
And close my eyes, lest I remember.

Lord, when I meet someone new,
someone who threatens me by his strangeness,
whose presence asks for adjustments,
whose ideas don't mesh with mine
and which shake the assumptions I wear
like a favourite jacket shaped to my comfort,
then help me to look,
not for his label, but for his humanity.
Not to close my mind, but to open my heart,
and see your presence in him.
Let me see you not just in my comfortable friends,
but in the eyes of strangers around me.
And Lord, help me to see
the only label that matters is love.
It's not always easy to recognise.
Sometimes it looks like a bloody crown.

The absent Samaritan

1 John 3:13-20

I'VE REWRITTEN the parable of the Good Samaritan. My version now reads:

> A man was on his way from Jerusalem down to Jericho when he fell in with robbers, who stripped him, beat him, and went off leaving him half dead. It so happened that a priest was going down by the same road; but when he saw him, he went past on the other side. So too a Levite came to the place, and when he saw him went past on the other side ... Then for a long time no one came. The sun beat down by day, the night was very cold, and the man died.
>
> (Luke 10 NEB, with additions)

I call it the Absent Samaritan. Because, for many people, help never comes. The Good Samaritan theme has inspired many folk to take a positive look at their neighbours, and has raised our understanding of who our neighbours are, but there's a dangerous assumption which often goes along with the theme. It's the danger of assuming that there always is a Good Samaritan, that somebody always does turn up to help the half-dead man. It's a comforting thought; the trouble is, it's not true. Too often the Samaritan never comes at all and people are left in their despair. The cry for help is blown away by the wind. I think about the life of our churches, and ourselves as believers. Are we fulfilling the Good Samaritan role, or acting out the Absent Samaritan? There are congregations which seem to be Good Samaritan Clubs, which all the GSs join only to help each other. There's a disturbing tendency in some groups these days so to emphasise that love must be shown within the fellowship (true enough!) that so much time goes in loving each other that it never seems to spill over onto the Jericho road, to the people waiting for the help that never comes. The whole point of the Good Samaritan thing is that it has to begin with me.

Wellesley Bailey's birthplace, Ireland Founder of TLM

It's hard to relate, Lord.
People in need. Millions of people.
Whether they're refugees, or leprosy sufferers, or people without food.
Living in countries I don't know.
Names I can't pronounce in languages I don't understand.
They're a long way away, just pictures.
Cardboard cutouts, with no more reality
than the picture on the back of a Kellogg's packet.
Even those nearer home are distant from my experience.
Statistics.
There's safety in numbers:
I can forget the humanity behind them.

Men, women, children, who feel, and laugh, and cry.
Not much laughter though, more crying.
Tears watering the parched ground, irrigating seeds of pain.
The only crop that grows in the desert.

I could hide behind the questions.
Why does it happen? Why so much suffering?
I could blame others. Politicians. Exploiters. Arms salesmen.
Multinational corporations. Currency manipulators.
That's fashionable – and true.
Why, Lord?
I hide behind the questions, and do nothing,
waiting for an answer, because I'm scared.
Overwhelmed. Frightened to get involved,
like turning away from a drunk in the gutter.

And who is my neighbour? I can't argue, Lord, I know.
And the Absent Samaritan? Yes, Lord, I know that too.
I know the answer has to begin with me.
Maybe I can't do a lot (more than I know, did you say?)
but I can do something.
Together with others, together with you I can spread your love around.
Show me how. So that through me, today,
someone may catch a glimpse of your love.
May find new life and hope.
May find the open door into your Kingdom.
And, Lord, as I pray for people in need, as I hear the crying far away,
let me not be deaf to the cry next door.

No easy way

Hebrews 12:1-2

W HEN PEOPLE learn that my major leisure activity is painting pictures, a common response is: "It must be very relaxing." Which shows how little many folk know about painting! It may be relaxing if your aims are not too high, but if you seriously want to accomplish something, then it's hard work. I occasionally spend a week painting with a professional painter. We spend eight to ten hours a day out in the open – wind, rain and sun, standing with our easels, analysing form and colour in landscape and trying to get it down in paint. "There is nothing between you and success," said John Rogers, the painter, "except what happens between your brush and the canvas." True. But brush and paint seem to have a life of their own and don't always conform to the painter's dream.

Last time, we had two other people with us – an elderly married couple who had a rather romantic dream of painting. They came thinking that they could learn a few rules of perspective, colour mixing and so on – a few tricks of the trade – to help them turn out competent paintings at will. It was painful for them as their illusions were slowly stripped away. The reality is that painting is a discipline which demands regular application, hard work and practice over the years if you are going to be able to communicate something worthwhile. I think they may have learned more about themselves than about painting in the week we were together.

The Christian life is the same, there is no easy way. Rules there are, as a foundation to build on, but you don't develop and grow just by following a set of rules. Discipline and hard work come in. Paul's reference to athletics is relevant: 'in a race all the runners run, but only one gets the prize ... but everyone goes into strict training' (1 Corinthians 9:24,25 NIV). 'Run with perseverance' says Hebrews 12:1.

Training and resolution are the requirements for anything worth doing – painting, language learning, athletics, Christian living. There are no short cuts. But that's not all. In painting, the greatest technician is cold unless he has a spark of sensitivity, perception, genius, to breathe life into what he creates. It's something which can't be measured or explained, but it can be recognised and accepted gladly when it's there. That's the Spirit. Whether inspiring the painter's vision or filling the Christian's life with joy, it is the Spirit who turns the pedestrian into the inspiring, who transforms the rules – the dead letter of the law – into life-giving freedom. God grant it to each one of us, together with the discipline to persevere.

Lord, they're not easy,
the demands you make.
You come into my life bringing joy and freedom and peace.
And it feels good.
But that's only the beginning.
Because along with that you ask for commitment.
For loyalty. Discipline.
For all my time and energy.
My abilities, to be used in your work.
I'm no longer my own, but yours.

I never know what will happen next
on the road you've shaped for me.
I only know you make demands.
For some it's martyrdom. Suffering.
For some it's publicity. Or politics.
Maybe that's a kind of martyrdom
for those who do it honestly.
For most of us
it's just the struggle to keep our balance
as we walk along the footpath of faith.

I can't see very far ahead.
Maybe that's just as well.
If I knew what was coming,
good or not so good,
I'd only worry, and try to change it.
Help me, Lord,
to put one step in front of the other
as I follow your lead.
I know you can.
Because wherever I go, you've already been.
Wherever I go, you are already there.
And with me on the journey.
It's good to know that, to experience it.
And Lord, help me to find the joy
that comes with answering your demands.
Help me to live the freedom
that comes from walking in your love.
Help me to know the peace
of your Spirit.

Stop and wait

Psalm 46

I REMEMBER SITTING quietly in my office one day – the labourers digging up the road outside with power drills having gone away to drink their lunch – and I began to look around the room. So often we take for granted the background in which we work. The office in which I worked was built in 1774, and my room contained a lovely 200-year-old fireplace. It was designed by the architects, the famous Adam brothers. The fireplace was all creamy white marble, beautifully proportioned. In the centre, a cherub was seated on a dolphin; there were graceful garlands of flower buds, and even several knots of ribbon, all carved from the stone. I'd always enjoyed antique furniture, yet, lovely though the fireplace was, I realised that I hadn't looked at it for weeks. When I was in the office, I was usually immersed in reading, writing, talking, thinking – even, on occasion, listening! Always busy. I knew the fireplace was there, and I'd have missed it if it had been taken away. I put papers on it. I even leaned on it sometimes if I were standing up and talking, but I hadn't really looked at it for some time. So I sat in front of the fireplace, and just gazed at it for three or four minutes. I realised how very nice it was, and after that, stayed conscious of its presence.

Maybe we take the Lord's presence for granted too. We believe He's 'there', present. We know it from experience, but we get so busy that we don't give ourselves time to step back and appreciate him. It's funny, isn't it, this being too busy for God, when you look at all the odd things we do find time for? And when we do find time for him it's often just to tell him what we want him to do, to deposit our ideas on him, or lean on him for support, like I lean on the fireplace. What we really need to do is to stop now and then in our busyness, relax, and wait for him. Learn to sit in his presence, and be aware of him. The poet, Ulrich Schaffer, writes*:

Suddenly the wheel of my life stops ...
... but then I notice your hands on the spokes
and my eyes are opened
to the life pulsing through the stillness
and my ears are opened
to the silence alive with you ...

'Be still, and know that I am God' (Psalm 46:10). Read it in context, the whole psalm. It speaks of earthquake and cataclysm, war and political upheaval. And in that context being still becomes a healing necessity, not a Saturday afternoon extra.

* From his book entitled *Into Your Light*, published by Inter-Varsity Press 1979

Lord, if only I had more time. Time for you.
Time to think and relax; to get to know you better.
Time to develop that relationship I need so much.
But I have time!
I'm sitting here now, writing, reading.
Maybe not for long, but it is time.
How shall I use it, Lord?
Shall I tune my thoughts from wavelength to wavelength,
filling my mind with an incoherent progression
of pointless words out of the air?
Or fine tune down to your presence?
Sometimes I'm happier listening to the undemanding
jumble of sound,
understanding nothing because I don't listen long enough.
Finding no word of meaning because I expect none.
Yet persuading myself that I'm in touch
with the world and with you
because my finger's on the dial,
and I'm constantly moving it around.

I fill my life with activity,
cluttering its corners with plans and programmes.
Convincing myself that what I'm doing
pleases you by its volume and repetition.
Telling everyone that it's your will
when I've not made the time to listen for it.

Help me push away the sound of traffic outside my window,
the mindless revving of engines,
the shouts of people. The crowded day.
Stop the wheel of my life a moment.
Put your divine spanner in the works, and make me pause.
Open my eyes to your presence.
Help me see the height and depth and breadth of your love.
The quiet, breathtaking beauty of it.

And then, Lord, what then?
Fill the silence once more with words?
No, Lord.
Maybe I'll just sit quietly with you.
Letting in your healing.
Thank you.

Commitment in prayer

Luke 22:39-46

SOME LITERATURE should carry a warning: 'This book can seriously damage your lifestyle. Don't read unless you are prepared to take it seriously.' I've just finished one – *School for Prayer* by Metropolitan Anthony. Anthony Bloom was the human head of the Russian Orthodox Church in Western Europe, and a well-known figure on television. His small book is deep and disturbing. He goes to the heart of prayer with an honesty and realism which are not all that common, and his insights make great demands.

'Words of prayer,' writes Anthony, 'have the quality of always being words of commitment' – if it's real prayer, that is. How often do we truly identify with our prayers? We pray for situations, for people, we ask God to intervene and act; and having prayed, we sit back, our duty done, waiting for results. But praying for something surely implies that we are prepared to stand with God in trying to achieve it. Shoulder to shoulder. The Good Samaritan (I wish he wouldn't crop up so often, he makes me feel guilty!) didn't hold a roadside prayer meeting and then walk on. He put the man on his horse ...

When we pray for peace, do our lives show the involvement – whether in human, social or political terms – which encourages peace? When we pray for healing, do we try to create the conditions of rest and change in which healing can take place? When we pray that the hungry may be fed, do we actually do anything? Or are we praying in a vacuum? I understand that sound waves don't travel in a vacuum. There are times when we pray instead of do, when we're perfectly capable of acting to put something right, but don't have the courage to do it. Times when we wrap prayer around us like insulating foam. Elsewhere in his book, Anthony says, 'It is absolutely pointless to ask God for something which we ourselves are not prepared to do'.

Sometimes, of course, we are truly powerless to achieve anything, except for prayer, but even then there still has to be that commitment. 'And being in anguish, he prayed more earnestly, and his sweat was like drops of blood falling to the ground' (Luke 22:44). Somehow, that doesn't describe my praying; how about yours? There are times when we need to take up our own cross, and not expect Christ to do it for us. Now that's not saying we should do things in our own strength. It's saying simply that the Lord expects us to develop our own sense of responsibility, and that it's often through action, fighting the good fight, that we prove his power with us. "I am with you, always" is a promise of presence, but not an undertaking to do it all for us. You may find the book hard to read, but you'll find it harder to forget.

Lord, sometimes I'm afraid to pray.
It scares me,
this whole business of talking to you.
Listening to you.
Who am I ...?
And what does it mean?
It's a heavy thing, Lord,
to be in contact with you.
It would be all right
if I could just use the passkey,
open the letterbox,
drop in my requests,
like a mail-order catalogue,
and wait for the parcel to come.

But when I pray
I hear you talking back to me.
I hear you saying
"You've used the words.
Now what are you going to do about it?"
Confronting, searching.
I think of Jesus, in the garden.
I catch a glimpse of what prayer meant to him.
Sweat ... like blood ...
Agonising, painful.
Prayer from the depths of his being
whether for others or himself.
Prayer beyond easy words.
Commitment.
To the cross. And beyond.

Lord, teach me to pray
in his name.
In his Spirit.
Not only believing prayer.
Not simply believing you'll do something about it.
But identifying prayer.
Putting myself into it,
standing alongside you, Lord
and committing myself to do all I can
to bring about what I'm praying for.

Lord, help me.
When I pray for peace, help me not to create dissension.
When I pray for my neighbour stir me up to help him.
When I pray 'Your kingdom come' inspire me to
share in its building.

Help me put my will where my mouth is,
And not to shift onto your shoulders
the things I can do something about myself.

Visions of Summer

Watercolour

Index in biblical order

TLM International
80 Windmill Road
Brentford
Middlesex TW8 0QH
United Kingdom
Tel: 020 8569 7292
Fax: 020 8569 7808
friends@tlmint.org
www.leprosymission.org

TLM Trading Limited
PO Box 212
Peterborough PE2 5GD
United Kingdom
Tel: 01733 239252
Fax: 01733 239258
enquiries@tlmtrading.com
www.tlmtrading.com

TLM Africa Regional Office
PO Box 11104
Hatfield
0028 Pretoria
Republic of South Africa
Tel: 27 12 349 2406 or
27 12 349 1904 x235
Fax: 27 12 349 2406

TLM Australia
PO Box 293
37 Ellingworth Parade
Box Hill
Victoria 3128
Australia
Tel: 61 39890 0577
Fax: 61 39890 0550
tlmaust@leprosymission
.org.au
www.leprosymission.org.au

TLM Belgium
(Leprazending)
PO Box 20
1800 Vilvoorde
Belgium
Tel: 32 22519983
Fax: 32 22519983
leprazending@online.be

TLM Canada
75 The Donway West
Suite 1410
North York
Ontario M3C 2E9
Canada
Tel: 1 416 4413618
Fax: 1 416 4410203
tlm@tlmcanada.org
www.tlmcanada.org

TLM Denmark
Skindergade 29 A1.
DK - 1159 Copenhagen
Denmark
Tel: 45 331 18642
Fax: 45 331 18645
lepra@lepra.dk
www.lepra.dk

TLM England & Wales,
Channel Islands & Isle
of Man
Goldhay Way
Orton Goldhay
Peterborough PE2 5GZ
United Kingdom
Tel: 01733 370505
Fax: 01733 404880
post@tlmew.org.uk
www.leprosymission.org.uk

TLM Finland
Hakolahdentie 32 A 4
00200 Helsinki
Finland
Tel: 358 9 692 3690
Fax: 358 9 692 4323
eeva-liisa.moilanen
@kolumbus.fi

TLM France
BP 186
63204 Riom Cedex
France
Tel: 33 473 387660
Fax: 33 473 387660

TLM Germany
Küferstrasse 12
73728 Esslingen
Germany
Tel: 49 711 353 072
Fax: 49 711 350 8412
LEPRA-Mission@t-online.de
www.lepramission.de

TLM Hong Kong
GPO Box 380
Central Hong Kong
Hong Kong
Tel: 85 228056362
Fax: 85 228056397
snelly@asiaonline.net

TLM Hungary
Alagi Ter 13
H-1151 Budapest
Hungary

TLM India Regional Office
CNI Bhavan
16 Pandit Pant Marg
Delhi 110 001
India
Tel: 91 11 371 6920
Fax: 91 11 371 0803
reception@tlm-india.org

TLM Italy
Via Adda 13
05100 Terni
Italy
Tel: 39 7448 11218
Fax: 39 7448 11218
agbertolino@librero.it

TLM Netherlands
Postbus 902
7301 BD Apeldoorn
Netherlands
Tel: 31 55 3558535
Fax: 31 55 3554772
leprazending.nl@inter.nl.net

TLM New Zealand
P O Box 10-227
Auckland
New Zealand
Tel: 64 9 630 2818
Fax: 64 9 630 0784
enquiries@tlmnz.org.nz

TLM Northern Ireland
Leprosy House
44 Ulsterville Avenue
Belfast BT9 7AQ
N Ireland
Tel: 01232 381937
Fax: 01232 381842
info@tlm-ni.org
www.tlm-ni.org

TLM Norway
PO Box 2347
Solli
Arbingst. 11N
0201 Oslo
Norway
Tel: 47 2243 8110
Fax: 47 2243 8730
gaute.hetland
@bistandsnemnda.no

TLM Portugal
Casa Adelina
Sitio do Poio
8500 Portimao
Portugal
Tel: 351 82 471180
Fax: 351 82 471516
coaa@mail.telepac.pt

TLM Republic of Ireland
5 St James Terrace
Clonskeagh Road
Dublin 6
Republic of Ireland
Tel: 353 126 98804
Fax: 353 126 98804
tlmroi@compuserve.com

TLM Scotland
89 Barnton Street
Stirling FK8 1HJ
Scotland
Tel: 01786 449 266
Fax: 01786 449 766
lindatodd@compuserve.com
www.biggar-net.co.uk
/tlmscotland

TLM South East Asia
6001 Beach Road
#08-06 Golden Mile Tower
199589 Singapore
Tel: 65 6 294 0137
Fax: 65 6 294 7663
pdsamson@tlmsea.com.sg

TLM Southern Africa
PO Box 46002
Orange Grove
2119 South Africa
Tel: 27 11 440 6323
Fax: 27 11 440 6324
leprosy@netactive.co.za

TLM Spain
Apartado de Correos
51.332 CP
28080 Madrid
Spain
Tel: 34 91 594 5105
Fax: 34 91 594 5105
mundosolidari
@mx3.redestb.es

TLM Sweden
Magasinsgatan 4
SE-692 37 Kumla
Sweden
Tel: 46 19 583790
Fax: 46 19 583741
lepra@algonet.se

TLM Switzerland
Chemin de Rechoz 3
CH-1027 Lonay/Vaud
Switzerland
Tel: 41 21 8015081
Fax: 41 21 8031948
mecl@bluewin.ch
www.lepramission.ch

TLM Zimbabwe
PO Box BE 200
Belvedere
Harare
Zimbabwe
Tel: 263 4 741817
tlmzim@tlmzim.icon.co.zw

ALM International
1 ALM Way
Greenville
S C 29601
USA
Tel: 1 864 271 7040
Fax: 1 864 271 7062
amlep@leprosy.org